The Methuen Book of Duologues for Young Actors

Anne Harvey trained at the Guildhall School of Music and Drama and now combines her work as an actress, writer and broadcaster with editing drama and poetry anthologies. She is also director of Pegasus, a company presenting literary programmes. She taught drama for many years and was a well-known adjudicator and examiner.

also available

The Methuen Book of Duologues for Young Actors

Edited with notes by
ANNE HARVEY

Preface by
IMOGEN STUBBS

Methuen Drama

For Leigh Hudson and Bess Jones,
who have inspired so many actors.

10 9

First published in Great Britain 1995
by Methuen Drama
Reissued with a new cover design 2002 by
Methuen Publishing Limited,
11–12 Buckingham Gate,
London SW1E 6LB

Copyright in the selection and editor's notes
© 1995, 2002 by Anne Harvey
Copyright in the preface © 1995, 2002 by Imogen Stubbs
The editor has asserted her moral rights

ISBN 10: 0–413–68900–X
ISBN 13: 978-0-413-68900-9

A CIP catalogue for this book
is available at the British Library

Typeset by Wilmaset Ltd, Birkenhead, Wirral
Printed and bound by Cox & Wyman Ltd, Reading, Berkshire

Caution

Contents

Preface

The great thing about a duologue is that there is always someone to blame if it doesn't work. My partner and I came bottom in a Speech and Drama competition rather spectacularly one year when – owing to an inordinate amount of ginger wine enlisted to help with nerves – she gave a passionate portrayal of Olivia (from *Twelfth Night*) with a cheeky, chirpy, cockney accent worthy of Dick Van Dyke, hummed the theme tune to 'Flipper' during my emotional bit and, on experiencing complete amnesia, chose to replace her final speech with the riveting spectacle of producing her bus ticket from her pocket and eating it. On another occasion, I lost the doorknob I had been using as a prop to accompany the line 'A doorknob' and presented my partner with a half-eaten Curly-Wurly, at which point we were overwhelmed by the kind of hysteria adjudicators never seem to find funny.

Obviously, pretending to be someone else talking to a person also pretending to be someone else can feel very silly and is most readily associated with children's games – or madness. It is so easy to feel ridiculous and so hard to be 'brave enough to make a fool of yourself'. And yet the only way to dignify the profession is to give yourself to it, as truthfully as you can, as a vehicle through which ideas and emotions are passed, so that the audience feels that what is feigned is not false. Above all, it requires teamwork – the sharing of personal opinion, experience and accumulated cultural baggage – to illuminate both the mysteries of the texts and the characters. This in turn requires diplomacy, patience, generosity, compassion, perseverance, mutual respect and the 'willing suspension of disbelief' to allow you and your fellow actors to take acting, and each other, seriously.

The duologue is a great training ground for this because most acting demands interacting and interdependence; and even if your partner is someone who confesses an inability to express any emotion since the day he sat on his gerbil, it has to be preferable to the partnerless situation in auditions where, as Simon Callow points out, self-conscious leads to a gradual lowering of the eye-line until the character being addressed invariably turns into Toulouse-Lautrec.

The disadvantage of a duologue is that you have only a few minutes to tell a story and arrest the audience – rather like a pop video. But you also have the possibility of tantalizing your public; what they have glimpsed through the keyhole should make them want to kick down the door! It is vital that both actors know the whole play intimately, listen to each other, and don't compete within it. Learning the lines early on allows you to respond in character to whatever surprising impulses are directed towards you in rehearsals. You cannot be fully creative or spontaneous with a book in your hand because the book easily becomes a security blanket and a barrier between you and your characterization and between you and your fellow actor. Do not be daunted by each other's inexperience. Nerves are all part of the job. 'Nervous?' 'I feel completely sick.' 'Quite right.' That is fine. What is unforgiveable is saying just before you go on (and, believe me, actors do) 'Are you really going to do that bit like that? Because it makes it impossible for me to do my part if you do yours like that.' Help each other with charm and tact and humour. This way, even if you fail as an actor, you'll succeed as a human being. And remember – going wrong is part of the thrill of live theatre and the source of all really delicious anecdotes. Oh! The injustice of it all.

Of course the choice of duologue is crucial and it has to be appropriate for both performers. Inevitably, within a drama class the students inherit characteristics which they may or may not really possess – the 'funny' bloke; tomorrow's Helen Mirren; the RSC type; the 'out-of-two-thousand-applicants-how-did-he-get-in?' – but define their position within the group. In duologues particularly, it is essential that the actors performing (and those in the audience) allow each other the confidence to try to locate other areas of themselves. Nowadays you can legitimately tackle anything, and discovering chameleon abilities through observation, instinct, and accent is not only necessary but liberating for most acting students. However, they must be people you can convincingly inhabit. Otherwise you descend into caricature and fairly certain and toe-curling humiliation – as when Jane Horrocks and I perversely attempted King Lear and Gloucester. Although playing against type feels more creative and is much more of a thrill to pull off, these days (alas) most casting is based on obvious strengths, not on faith in the unknown.

With this in mind, Anne Harvey has compiled a wonderful selection of pieces for young actors – immensely varied in tone and style and offering a cornucopia of characters while still remaining feasible. Moreover, they are not the hackneyed, over-used pieces I remember digging out of the library, which invariably prompted our teachers to rapturous descriptions of famous actors who had played the roles definitively and made our own paltry attempts seem a desecration of the memory. They are deftly chosen for their unfamiliarity and this is a great bonus – it allows the actor to unleash his or her prodigious imagination on the scene and ensures a far greater likelihood of the audience or examiner staying awake.

There are wonderful opportunities for both girls and boys to discover how to play children without being twee. From the passionate comic seven-year-olds in Willy Russell's *Blood Brothers*; middle-class Kate and the streetwise Rosie in Vivian Alcock's *The Cuckoo Sister* and the slightly older teenagers in Ian Hamilton Finlay's *Walking Through Seaweed* (good idea to swop parts in these scenes during rehearsals); to Jan in Serraillier's *The Silver Sword*, where there is the added fun of learning how to work with animals.

For female actors there is the immensely rewarding challenge of proving that comic characters exist outside French and Saunders, thanks to Moliere, Sheridan, Eliot, Coward, Storey, Frayn and less familiar writers like Lisa Evans. I would relish the prospect of playing any one of the characters in *Split Down the Middle*, *Stamping, Shouting and Singing Home*, or *Walking Through Seaweed*. There are also the equally fulfilling but gruelling roles like Shaw's Joan, Effie in *Effie's Burning*, Rose in *The Sea* and Martha in *The Children's Hour*. These require a combination of daring and restraint and, needless to say, teamwork – they are not solo flings.

For male actors, there are lots of enviable 'laddish' pieces with footballs and swearwords and plenty of opportunities to show-off that you can talk and move at the same time (a great asset unless you want to be a newscaster) – Jonathan Harvey's enchanting *Beautiful Thing* (this also has the joy of requiring Cagney and

Lacey imitations), *Two Weeks with the Queen* by Mary Morris, *A Game of Soldiers* by Jan Needle, and *The Goalkeeper's Revenge* – a terrific play adapted from Bill Naughton. For delirious absurdity, there are scenes by Dario Fo and Ken Campbell and more reflective roles include the characters in *Journey's End* (a potentially devastating piece about the First World War), the Russian and English boys fighting over an egg in *Across Oka* (a great training in mishandling props), and Alan in one of my favourite scripts *P'tang, Yang, Kipperbang*. All the scenes offer the pitfalls of over-acting, botched timing, misjudged humour and staggering lapses of taste. But equally, there is every chance that you will surprise everyone – including yourself. It is amazing how many different people there are inside you when you know how to access them.

You will never again have the chance to explore quite so many characters in so short a space of time (unless weekly rep returns with a vengeance), so do relish it. After all, the partner you blame may turn out to be the next Ken Branagh.

Imogen Stubbs
London, 1995

Notes to the Actor

It was seeing Imogen Stubbs play St Joan that made me invite her to write an introduction for this book. Her tough yet tender interpretation of one of the most coveted heroines in English drama was utterly convincing and entirely memorable. As you can read, she rates 'conviction' very high on her list of essentials for an actor.

Having been an adjudicator and examiner, I recognise the situations she describes all too well. I can remember many occasions when I sat, pen poised, waiting for embarassed young students to gain control of their giggles (and their senses) . . . Highly amusing for themselves, but leaving the jaded judge unimpressed! When I was a teacher, my own pupils could suffer similar lapses and most professional actors and teachers can recall uncomfortable moments on stage. But those who are serious will live through the worst of times and emerge ready to learn, and the introduction is packed with ideas and advice.

Duologues have been part of my life for a very long time. I acted my first one at the age of eight and still know it by heart. It was from Maurice Maeterlinck's *The Bluebird*, one of many 'hack-neyed over-used pieces' rather like the ones Imogen Stubbs recalls; others are from *Peter Pan*, *Toad of Toad Hall*, *Alice in Wonderland* and *The Brontës* . . . with some of the most unsuitably cast Toads and Alices one can imagine. It was such lack of choice for young actors that led me to compile anthologies of drama material in the first place. I think it so important that teachers and pupils are aware of the range of literature, from different periods and cultures, and of ways of using language. Of course the old 'chestnuts' have a place and are always new to someone. It was, after all, *The Bluebird* that gave me a start in discovering the skills needed in acting, amongst them timing, use of pause, listening and

– so high on the list – spontaneity. And I have a lurking feeling that 'the doorknob' to which Imogen refers is in that evergreen scene from *Tom Sawyer*, between poor Tom and the precocious Becky!

I am so glad that she mentions the importance of reading the entire play, and I'm going to repeat it. A short scene can only tell you so much. You will only grasp the author's intentions and understand characters and situations when you have read, re-read and re-read *again*, the *whole* play.

A bonus in reading these plays is that most of them offer other, equally tempting, duologues. An editor is limited over space and many scenes had to be cut because the anthology grew too long. I made the decision to exclude excerpts from plays already included in *The Methuen Audition Book for Young Actors*, many of which did have some excellent two-handers – as you will perhaps have discovered from your reading. In my own student acting days, in teaching, examining and adjudicating, the duologue experience was always one of the happiest and most rewarding. I hope those who use this book in performance, or for reading, will agree.

Anthologies like this take a huge amount of work, and certainly not all mine. This collection could not have happened without the enthusiasm, care and support of two excellent editors: thank you, Peggy Butcher and Sarah Hulbert.

Anne Harvey

Anne Boleyn
Peter Albery

Henry VIII's first wife, Katherine of Aragon, confronts her husband's mistress, Anne Boleyn, in the Royal Palace at Greenwich. Katherine, in her mid-forties, plump, pious and determined to keep Henry, speaks broken English with a Spanish accent. Anne, vivacious and attractive, in her late twenties, is desperate to legalise her relationship with the King.

Although this play is now out of print, the situation is well-known and the historical background well documented.

Time: 1529.

KATHERINE (*to* ANNE). You wished to speak with me?

ANNE (*a little taken aback*). Er – yes – it would be as well.

KATHERINE (*proudly*). As well?

ANNE. It ill becomes you, Madam, to be haughty.

KATHERINE. If you would keep your place as the king's concubine –

ANNE. Concubine! I am not – (*She checks.*)
How dare you!

KATHERINE. That is what all Europe calls you.
If it is wrong I am sorry.
But you are surely not his wife.

ANNE. Madam, I came to spare you.
To appeal to your better self to renounce this man
Who no longer loves you.
And to retire with honour and dignity
As dowager Princess of Wales.

Are you determined to risk the future
Of your daughter Mary?
I warn you the king's patience is cut to the quick.
Any further resistance will only madden him.

KATHERINE. I do not understand you.
It is the future of my daughter that I protect
By refusing consent to this lie.

ANNE. There is no future, Madam, for those that are dead.

KATHERINE (*after a pause*). You say that to frighten me.
The king would never permit it.

ANNE. To live in the past is a dangerous delusion, Madam.
Henry has empowered me to say
That he does not wish to see you here
On our return from Windsor in a month's time.

KATHERINE. More lies.
If it were true, he would tell me so himself.

ANNE. It is true.

KATHERINE. Then it was said by a Henry
Who is not *my* Henry.

ANNE. Precisely, dowager Princess.

KATHERINE. Listen, you foolish girl;
Some men are dual by nature.
My Henry is generous and brave and trusting,
But he harbours an *alter ego*
That I have learned to seal in slumber.
It is vicious, crafty and cruel.
As long as I am here at the palace
My love will control this spirit.
But if you tamper with the seal
And banish its guardian,
God help you, and God help all of us.

ANNE. You would try to retaliate;
To frighten me with a witch's cauldron.
I can hold the king in my arms
And at my feet if I will:
Can you?

KATHERINE. I am contented to hold him in my heart.

ANNE. You hold nothing but a phantom;
You are old, unlovely and unwanted.
Am I to inform the king that you disobey him?

KATHERINE (*suddenly weary*). I do not know. I have tried
to help you.
Let him confirm it in his own hand.

ANNE. You choose to doubt my word?

KATHERINE (*motioning her to go*). If you please, I am tired
after my drive.

ANNE (*handing her a note*). Perhaps you recognise this
hand,
Giving me authority to search your chambers?

KATHERINE (*reading*). It is incredible.

ANNE. Yes, the *alter ego*. I am afraid I removed the seal.

KATHERINE. You fool, you blind, unhappy little fool.
That is why you are here.
No wonder you thirst to be queen.
Fear already pickets your bones.

ANNE. A thirst that shall soon be assuaged.
I came in kindness to give you a last warning,
If the Pope will not grant dispensation
We shall settle this matter in May.

KATHERINE. You will still be Henry's concubine in
Europe.

ANNE. You shall crawl to me for that.

3

KATHERINE. It is all so childish and futile.
Why do you wish to search my rooms?

ANNE. Because someone has stolen the king's love-letters
to me.

KATHERINE. You surely do not think that I –

ANNE. You should not protest. I might doubt *your* word.

KATHERINE. This is fantastic! Does Henry forget
That I am the daughter of a king,
And aunt to the Holy Roman Emperor,
That he subjects me to such treatment
From a wanton without manners or degree?
(*Going to door.*) I shall complain to the king myself.

ANNE. I should save your limbs, he is out hunting.

KATHERINE. Then I will wait till he returns.

ANNE. Wait, yes, you may well learn to wait.
It is all you will have to do in future.

The Cuckoo Sister
Vivien Alcock

Kate, aged 11, is haunted by the knowledge that, thirteen years ago, her parents' first daughter, Emma, was snatched from her pram and never returned. Now it seems that 13-year-old Rosie, who has come to stay, could be the real Emma . . . although she does not fit Kate's idea of her lost sister. Rosie is smart and streetwise, with a very different background and upbringing from middle-class Kate. She is in bed when Kate comes in, distressed and soaking wet from running through the rain.

Time: The present.

ROSIE. You washed your hair? (*Thrusting something under pillow.*)

KATE. No. I went for a walk.

ROSIE. In all the wet?

KATE. I was running away.

ROSIE. You ain't serious?

KATE. No. It was a joke. Here's your milk.

ROSIE. Ta. I nearly run away once. Got my bags packed and everything. Then I thought – where the hell am I going? Nowhere. So I hid out on Hockley Station, down on the platform, just to make Mum worried. I meant to stay out late but it was draughty and there were drunks, and I'd finished my book, so I went back. She was still out so she never knew nothing. Just as well. She'd have been worried sick . . . she would, you know.

5

KATE. Mummy would cry her eyes out if I ran away. She'd probably have a nervous breakdown.

ROSIE (*fumbling under pillow for letter*). If I show you something, you won't tell, will you?

KATE. No. I promise.

ROSIE. It's a letter from my mum. It ain't to me, it's to one of her friends. Bettine. She works at the launderette and she give it to me. Mum's got married.

KATE (*who knows this already*). Married? Has she? Who to?

KATE. She don't say. Ain't put no address neither. D'you want to see it? Here . . . be careful . . . don't tear it, mind. . . .

KATE (*reading*). dear bettine, i am sorry i went off without saying goodbye but i was in a state i had to give rosie back to her people you see she wos never my baby reely . . . i was just minding her i had no choice it was only rite now for the good news i am married he is a good man. . . . (*Finishes the letter silently.*)

ROSIE (*anxious*). What do you think? D'you think she was crying about me?

KATE. Crying? I didn't notice . . .

ROSIE. Yeh. There, see. . . . (*Points to letter.*)

KATE (*looking*). I wos crying and my maskara run . . .

ROSIE. Says she wanted to send me her bouquet. I wish she had. It'd be something . . . something to . . .

KATE. Rosie, don't –

ROSIE. I ain't crying. I ain't crying over HER.

KATE (*re-reading parts*). I wos in a state . . . i had no choice . . . it was only rite . . . (*She looks up to see* ROSIE *watching her.*)

ROSIE. Mum's a terrible liar, you know. She'll say anything that suits her. It don't mean it's true. She's made up of lies – even her own name. You know what your dad thinks. That it ain't really Martin at all and that's why he couldn't find no record. You don't want to believe a word she says. Look, there's a lie right there. Making out she's a child-minder.

KATE. I suppose she couldn't very well say that. . . .

ROSIE. That she stole me out of your mum's pram.

KATE. Yes.

ROSIE. D'you think it's true then?

KATE. It might be.

ROSIE (*shouting*). Might be! That ain't good enough. I want to KNOW! (*A crash of thunder outside.*) I can't be Emma, I can't. I been Rosie too long. I'll always be Rosie.

KATE. We could go on calling you Rosie. I'm sure Mummy wouldn't mind.

ROSIE. Oh Gawd, you're such a kid. I didn't mean . . . I dunno what I meant. It's like . . . I can't be somebody's lost baby. I been a baby. I done all that with mum. Cut my teeth, had chicken pox and measles, fell off my friend's bike, the lot. I'm thirteen now, that's nearly grown-up. I can't change back just to suit your mum. And it's not as if the rest of you wanted me.

KATE. How do you mean?

ROSIE. I ain't stupid. Your dad's been kind and all that, but he won't never be happy not knowing. Every time I do

7

something wrong, he'll be thinking, 'She ain't one of us.'
And your Mrs Trapp don't fool me with her 'dearies'. She
couldn't find her purse last week and you should've seen the
way she looked at me. 'You haven't seen it, have you dearie?
I know I put it on the table and it's not there now'. And all
the time it was in her shopping bag. She thinks I'm a thief.
She's always watching me. She nearly wets her pants when I
go near them silver candlesticks on the sideboard. And as for
you –

KATE. What about me?

ROSIE. You're a bleeding little snob, aren't you?

KATE. I'm not!

ROSIE (*shrugging*). Oh, you ain't said nothing. But I seen
the look on your face like I was a bad smell.

KATE. That's not fair. I've been jolly kind to you.

ROSIE. Kind! (*Shouting.*) Yeh, you've all been kind, and I
hope it chokes you. (*A flash of lightning and a clap of thunder
terrify* KATE.) You're not frightened of thunder are you?

KATE. A bit.

ROSIE. Like my mum. She hates it . . . Hey, that was a big
bang, Kate. It's all right, silly. It can't hurt you, you know.

KATE (*trembling*). The lightning can. It can strike you
dead.

ROSIE. Not indoors. It can't reach us in here. . . . Cheer
up, kid. It'll soon be over. Your hair's drying rough. I'll
brush it for you. (KATE *passes her a brush.*) It's still a bit
damp. You must've got soaked. There, that's better. . . .
Was you really trying to run away?

KATE. Not really. I just wanted to be on my own for a bit.
8

ROSIE. Yeh. I know. . . . (*She folds her letter over and over into a small square. The storm has passed.*) I wish I knew 'oo she's married. I didn't think she 'ad no new boy-friend. She never spoke of one . . . If she's married that fat pig, I'll kill her.

KATE. Who?

ROSIE. That Harry Jenkins. Remember, I told you about him.

KATE. The one who got drunk?

ROSIE. Yeh. And broke her bingo vase.

KATE. I thought you said she'd thrown him out.

ROSIE. I only hope she threw him far enough.

KATE (*a pause. KATE is uneasy*). What does he look like?

ROSIE. Horrible. Huge. Fat. Hairy. Like a blooming red ape.

KATE (*who met him when she was out in the rain, shivers*). I think I've seen him. (*Slowly.*) I think he's looking for you.

ROSIE. Him? Harry Jenkins? You're dreaming, kid. If he's married Mum, he won't want me hanging around. He knows what I think of him. If he's married Mum . . .' (*Turns her face away.*)

KATE (*awkwardly*). I ought to be going down. I promised Mummy I'd lay the table. Is there anything I can get you?

ROSIE. No, ta very – I mean, thanks most awfully.

KATE (*suddenly bursting out*). I don't mean to be a snob!

ROSIE. No. Sorry. It ain't your fault. . . . They don't know what it's like do they? They don't know what it's like for us. You and me, we're right in the middle of it. They think it's their problem, but it ain't. It's ours.

9

The Sea
Edward Bond

The entire community of an East Coast village is affected by the drowning of a young man, Colin. Rose, a young girl, was engaged to marry Colin; and Willy, his close friend, was with him at the time of the accident. Bond says, 'We even need a sense of tragedy . . . tragedy as something to use in our lives, that gives us sympathy and understanding of other people.' The scene is set on the beach, where Colin's body is upstage, half in the water.

Time: 1907.

Beach.

The stage is empty except for a body upstage. It is covered with trousers, socks, vest and jersey – all dark. There are no shoes. The jersey is pulled up over the head and the arms, which are lifted up and bent at the elbows in the act of removing the jersey – so the jersey forms a hood covering the head, neck, shoulders, arms and hands. The dark vest covers the trunk. The top half of the body is on the beach and the rest in the water.

ROSE comes on. She is looking ahead at someone who has gone on in front of her.

ROSE (*calling ahead*). I must sit down. (*She sits.*)

WILLY comes on from the direction in which she shouted.

WILLY. Are you all right?

ROSE. Yes.

WILLY. Shall I leave you alone?

ROSE. Yes.

WILLY (*nods. Slight pause*). I don't like to. You haven't been out here since he drowned.

ROSE (*remotely*). I'll see you back at the house.

WILLY. All right. (*Pause. WILLY doesn't move.*)

ROSE. This stupid inquest.

WILLY. Why? (*Pause.*)

ROSE. The coroner will say he's sorry and decide why he died. Why? You might as well have an inquest on birth. They're afraid of me. I'm touched by death. Perhaps you are. I see it when they call to say they're sorry. They look at me as if I'm a dangerous animal they have to pat . . .

WILLY. You're supposed to forget what they look like very soon. It comes as a shock. But it's hard to forget the voice. You suddenly hear that twenty years later.

ROSE. Really they come to be calmed and assured. I have to find some of my pain to share with them. A taste. Then they know that if I can bear it so can they when it comes.

WILLY. He knew more about sailing than I do. But we both knew it was wrong to be out. He wanted to get here quickly. To see you. Perhaps he wanted to show something. I mean: prove. (*Shrugs.*) I said let's go back. I kept asking, 'How close is the land?' He didn't answer. He went on working. Pulling ropes. And he baled water in a bucket. He knew we'd made a mistake. It was dangerous to be there.

ROSE. What did he say?

WILLY. Nothing. Then the boat turned over. I saw the bottom coming up out of the water. It looked very ugly. It was wet and suddenly smooth in all that chaos. I yelled but I couldn't hear him. He was gone. (*Pause.*) Did you love him . . . a great deal?

ROSE. What?

WILLY. I thought perhaps he wasn't sure. I mean about what you felt. It was clear what he felt.

ROSE. Why are you saying this?

WILLY. Somehow, he was afraid. That was so unnatural for him. He was sure and firm about everything else. It seems terrible that he could be afraid . . . I think that would have destroyed him. A hero's fear.

ROSE. Fear?

WILLY. You were brought up together. Your aunt wanted you to marry. Everyone knew you would. It was too easy. He was afraid one day you'd meet another man – perhaps even a weaker man – and he'd lose you. A hero must be afraid of weaker men.

ROSE. Why?

WILLY. He never talked of you. No photographs. I didn't know what you looked like. Sometimes he said he'd written or you'd been somewhere. Of course I'd formed my own picture of you.

ROSE. How long did you know him?

WILLY. Seven years. I'm twenty-one. We were the same age. (*Silence.*)

ROSE. If I'd seen him die it would be easier to forget him. I can see him working and not saying anything. Wet to the skin. And the noisy sea. But I can't see him when he dies. (*Pause.*) He was very beautiful. He had dark eyes. I think of him as a fire.

WILLY. Why?

ROSE. A fire that doesn't die out. I've seen it burn in the sea.

WILLY. What d'you mean?

ROSE. When we were young we lit fires on the beach. At night. The fire shone on his face. I saw it reflected in the sea. It danced because both the flames and the water moved.

WILLY. D'you feel anything wrong?

ROSE. You mean guilty?

WILLY. Yes. When someone dies people sometimes –

ROSE. No. I was always happy with him. There was nothing mean and selfish in it. It seemed perfect. Now I have nothing to live for. There's nothing to look forward to. I don't know what I shall do. I can't think of anything to make one day pass. Yet I have most of my life to live. I don't know how I shall get through it. He was the only person who could understand me now.

WILLY. I understand you a little.

ROSE. Yes, but what does that matter to me?

WILLY. All people matter to each other.

ROSE. That isn't true, of course.

WILLY. No. (*Silence*).

ROSE. I can't bear to lose him. I don't think I can live without him.

WILLY (*quiet anger*). I think that love can be a terrible disaster. And hope is sometimes pride and ambition. When I'm lost in darkness I'll shut my eyes and feel my way forward, grope like an animal, not be guided by some distant light.

ROSE. How can you escape from yourself, or what's happened to you, or the future? It's a silly question. It's

13

better out here where he died. At home there's so much to do. People coming and going. Why? What does it matter to them? How can I escape from *that*?

WILLY. If you look at life closely it is unbearable. What people suffer, what they do to each other, how they hate themselves, anything good is cut down and trodden on, the innocent and the victims are like dogs digging rats from a hole, or an owl starving to death in a city. It is all unbearable but that is where you have to find your strength. Where else is there?

ROSE. An owl starving in a city.

WILLY. To death. Yes. Wherever you turn. So you should never turn away. If you do you lose everything. Turn back and look into the fire. Listen to the howl of the flames. The rest is lies.

ROSE. How just. How sane.

WILLY *stands and looks upstage.*

ROSE. What is it?

WILLY. He's on the beach. There. (ROSE *and* WILLY *go up to the body.*)

ROSE. Why is he like that?

WILLY. He tried to pull the jumper over his head. So he could swim.

ROSE. He drowned.

WILLY. Yes. (*They stare silently for a moment.*)

ROSE. Is it him?

WILLY. Yes. I know his clothes. Go and fetch Mr Evens. I'll keep watch.

14

ROSE. Yes. (ROSE *hurries out. After a moment* WILLY *crouches down by the body.*)

WILLY (*coldly*). How will they get you into the box? You're a corpse and they'll break your arms. They'll cut your clothes and fold you up like a dummy. What's on your face now? Is it quiet, or swollen, or scratched?

Skungpoomery
Ken Campbell

*'Skungpoomery' – thinking up a word and then doing it – happens after
the opening scene between the Wibbles in this zany farce. Here PC
Nicholas Wibble, who has become rather a 'Mummy's boy', is being
mothered (or smothered) by his dominating mother. Mrs Wibble could
quite easily be played by a male actor.*

Time: The present.

PC NICHOLAS WIBBLE. But all the other policemen
wear boots.

MRS WIBBLE. That's because they haven't got nice
sandals.

WIBBLE. Well why've I always got to be different.

MRS WIBBLE. It's not a case of 'being different', Nicholas, it's a case of being sensible. It's unhealthy to have your
feet laced up inside those big clumping boots all day in the
hot weather –

WIBBLE. O Mum.

MRS WIBBLE. I don't want to hear any more about it,
Nicholas.

WIBBLE. Anyway those sandals pinch my feet, Mum.

MRS WIBBLE. Nicholas! You little fibber! We got those
sandals at Clarks and we both looked down the X-Ray
machine together and we both saw that you had plenty of
room in those sandals. Nicholas!

WIBBLE. Wh-at?

MRS WIBBLE. What's that?

WIBBLE. What's what?

MRS WIBBLE. On your tie?

WIBBLE. Nothing.

MRS WIBBLE. Egg dribblings. Look at that. And I all nicely ironed it yesterday morning and now you've dribbled your egg on it. Come here. (*She leads him by his tie to the bowl and cloth.*)

WIBBLE. O Mum.

MRS WIBBLE. O and it's not coming out look. It'll have to be put in soak.

WIBBLE. Oh no, Mum – look I'm due on the beat in five minutes. I can't wait while you soak it.

MRS WIBBLE. Well I'm certainly not letting you go out with your tie in that state.

WIBBLE. The Sergeant gets really cross if I'm late.

MRS WIBBLE. Well you'll just have to wear your bow-tie.

WIBBLE. O no.

MRS WIBBLE. Nicholas!

WIBBLE. O look all the other policemen wear ordinary straight ties.

MRS WIBBLE. Come here and let's put it on you and have less of your nonsense. Your Aunty Glad gave you this nice bow tie – and did you write her a proper thank you letter?

WIBBLE. Yes.

MRS WIBBLE. Good boy. (*Looking at his face.*) Hanky? (*He supplies it.*) Lick. (*He licks it and she wipes a bit of dirt off his face with it.*)

WIBBLE. 'Bye then, Mum.

MRS WIBBLE. Kiss please. I've done you some sandwiches.

WIBBLE. O Mum, can't I eat in the canteen with the other policemen?

MRS WIBBLE. O you make me so cross, Nicholas. We've just managed to nearly get rid of all your spots and now you want to go into that nasty canteen and eat greasy fried stuff.

WIBBLE. It's not all greasy fried stuff in there, Mum.

MRS WIBBLE. You're an ungrateful boy, Nicholas.

WIBBLE. O I'm not ungrateful at all, Mum. I'm grateful. I really am. It's all right. I'll take the sandwiches. And I'll enjoy them.

MRS WIBBLE. I should think so. O Nicholas! I ironed those trousers at the weekend and now look at them. They're all baggy at the knees. Don't you hitch them up when you sit down?

WIBBLE. Yes.

MRS WIBBLE. Take them off and let me give them a quick press.

WIBBLE. O no, Mum – look I'm going to be ever so late now.

MRS WIBBLE. Take them off, Nicholas, it won't take a moment.

WIBBLE. No.

MRS WIBBLE. Nicholas!!!

WIBBLE. Oooooooooooh! (*Stamp and paddy.* MRS WIBBLE *waits. He sulkily removes his trousers revealing*
18

Chilprufe underpants. MRS WIBBLE *takes the trousers off and returns with an iron and an ironing board.*)

MRS WIBBLE. Right.

WIBBLE. Please hurry up, Mum.

MRS WIBBLE. I'm being as quick as I can, Nicholas. (*She is now ironing.*) The number of times I've been on to you, Nicholas, to just think before you go to bed at night, what you're going to need in the morning, and go over it and check it's all right then; there's absolutely no need for this breakfast time misery. But you, you never seem to know what you're at or what you're doing. (*The phone rings. She answers the iron, holding it next to her ear.*) Hello? Hello? Yahhhhhhhhhhhhhhh! (*In her agony, she puts the iron down on the trousers.*) Butter! Get the butter, Nicholas!

WIBBLE. Oh yes, here you are. (*He shoves a full round soft marge pack onto his Mum's ear. They tie the pack to her ear with a scarf.*)

MRS WIBBLE. Nicholas, you will be the death of me!

WIBBLE. How's it my fault, Mum. If you stick the iron in your ear.

MRS WIBBLE. Nicholas, just shut up! (*Clouts him.*) Ooooof. (*The pain of the burn.*) Go and answer it.

WIBBLE (*picking up the phone*). That's all right. That's not so good. That's very good. That's just first class. That's awful. That's good. That's rotten.

MRS WIBBLE. Who is it?

WIBBLE. It's Auntie Glad. She wanted some help sorting out her tomatoes. O no! O Mum look what you've done now! (*He picks up the trousers revealing a huge burn hole.*) O no.

19

MRS WIBBLE. I'm not the least bit sympathetic, Nicholas. It's just a direct result of your own thoughtlessness.

WIBBLE. What am I going to do now?

MRS WIBBLE. Well you'll just have to wear your shorts.

WIBBLE. O no!

MRS WIBBLE. They're in the airing cupboard.

WIBBLE. I can't wear short trousers on the beat, Mum!

MRS WIBBLE. Of course you can. It's a nice warm morning. Go and get them before I get very cross indeed. I don't know how I'm going to mend these. They'll need the most enormous patch. O come along. Let's get you out of the house. (*She goes off and returns immediately with the shorts*). Get into those and off you go. Then I can have a cup of tea in peace.

WIBBLE (*miserably and slowly dons his shorts*). This is going to be the worst day of my life. (*Goes.*)

MRS WIBBLE. And he's forgotten his sandwiches. (*She walks off.*)

Split Down the Middle
David Campton

Two girls, in their late teens or early twenties, are adrift in a rowing boat at sea in a fog, during their works' outing. Josie is described as small, thin and sharp; Fran as rather large and slow. They begin to panic and to hope that someone will hear Fran's attempt at hooting.
   Time: The present.

FRAN. HOOT . . . HOOT . . . HOOT. . . .

JOSIE. Shut up.

FRAN. Thanks, Josie. I was just about giving up.

JOSIE. I'm not cracking. We've got to keep our heads.

FRAN. Do you think we're near the end of the pier, Josie?

JOSIE. Do you?

FRAN. You'll feel a lot better when we're tucking in to hot pie and chips with a steaming pot of tea, and bread and butter and jam and cakes.

JOSIE. Don't. . . . When I had my palm read she couldn't see a boy in my immediate future. Now I know why.

FRAN. Funny how you think of things like that.

JOSIE. Hear me laughing.

FRAN. Takes it out of you, hooting does. Are you going to take over?

JOSIE. No.

FRAN. I bet you're a better hooter than me.

JOSIE. What's the use. Face facts.

FRAN. Would you like me to hoot again? Just in case anybody's passing?

JOSIE. NO. If we're going, let's go in peace.

FRAN. Do you know what I'm going to do then? Do you? I'm going to wait till it's dark, really dark. Then I'm going to strike matches.

JOSIE. What matches?

FRAN. I know it ought to be rockets, but we haven't got any rockets. I've got a box of matches though. I always keep a box with me in case. In my handbag. Here. (*Feels under seat.*)

JOSIE. It might help. Yes, it might just. Clever old Fran. Don't listen to people when they tell you that you're dim, Fran. You have some bright ideas. Every so often. Of course I'd have thought of striking matches myself if I'd brought a box with me. But I didn't, so there wasn't any point in thinking. Let's strike one now.

FRAN. Josie . . .

JOSIE. It's nearly dark enough. . . .

FRAN. Josie . . .

JOSIE. Just in case anybody's looking this way.

FRAN. Josie . . .

JOSIE. What?

FRAN. I can't.

JOSIE. Can't what?

FRAN. Strike a match.

JOSIE. Did you forget your matches? Trust you.

FRAN. I've got them here.

JOSIE. What are you worried about, then?

FRAN. They're wet. They won't strike when they're wet.

JOSIE. Trust you to put them where they'd get wet. Trust you.

FRAN. I put them in my handbag. It's full of water now.

JOSIE. Trust you to put your handbag where it could fill with water. Trust you.

FRAN. Under the seat was dry when I put my bag there.

JOSIE. Think ahead. Trust you not to think ahead.

FRAN. When I felt under my seat just now, my bag was floating.

JOSIE. Floating?

FRAN. In water.

JOSIE. Trust you.

FRAN. Under my seat. Water.

JOSIE (*blankly*). Water?

FRAN. Sea water. Under my seat. My bag floating. Do you know what I think, Josie? I think . . .

JOSIE. WE'RE LEAKING.

FRAN. That's what I think.

JOSIE. Going down.

FRAN. Not just yet.

JOSIE. And it's all your fault, you great gorm. Not satisfied with dragging me out into the middle of the ocean. Oh no. You have to pick a boat with a hole in it.

FRAN. It's not filling very fast.

23

JOSIE. Sitting here waiting for the water to rise. It's torture. If we had any sense we'd jump overboard and finish ourselves quick.

FRAN. I could empty us a bit with my handbag.

JOSIE. Your handbag!

FRAN. It's sopping already. The water can't do any more damage.

JOSIE. Can't it? You wait till we start breathing it.

FRAN. Don't give up hope, Josie.

JOSIE. I gave up hope hours ago. Then you had to bring it back with your chattering about matches. Now I'll have to give up all over again.

FRAN. You're not crying, are you, Josie?

JOSIE (*in tears*). I don't want to die.

FRAN. Rotten way to end a day's outing. I wonder if we could get the money back on our return halves? Wipe your eyes, Josie . . . I'd lend you my hanky but it's in my handbag. Shush . . . shush. . . . You're a big girl now.

JOSIE. I'm too young to die. I haven't lived yet.

FRAN. Make the most of what you've got while you've got it. That's what I say.

JOSIE. What have we got left?

FRAN. Well, we're together, aren't we?

JOSIE. Some comfort.

FRAN. We're friends, Josie. At least you're among friends.

JOSIE. My feet are cold.

FRAN. Josie . . .

JOSIE. What?

FRAN. Should we sing a hymn?

JOSIE. What do you want to sing a hymn for?

FRAN. Might make us feel better about . . .

JOSIE (*Wails*) . . .

FRAN. I saw a picture once. At the pictures. Christians sang hymns before they were thrown to the lions. It made them feel a lot happier. A hymn might make you feel happier. 'Onward Christian Soldiers' . . . or 'For those in Peril on the Sea'.

JOSIE. You're insensitive. That's what you are.

FRAN. I was just trying to make you feel happier about going. Would you rather we sang something brighter? 'Roll out the Barrel' or 'You are my Sunshine'?

JOSIE. If we got balloons and paper hats, we could have a party.

FRAN. Not just before going down. I don't think that would be right.

JOSIE. You're not going to see me scared. I'm not going to give you the satisfaction.

FRAN. That's right. Buck up.

JOSIE. Shut up. . . . My feet are wet . . . I can feel my stockings clinging to my toes. . . . Why don't you say something?

FRAN. They're going to miss us . . . the girls in the shop. I bet they have a collection. . . . I bet we have a smashing wreath. They could float it after us . . . out to sea. . . . (JOSIE *sobs*.) I'm doing my best to cheer you up, Josie. . . .

25

The water's not much higher . . . we could have hours yet. . . . (JOSIE *wails*.) You live your life all over again just . . . before . . . at least, somebody once said you live your life all over again. . . . We'll be going through some times again, won't we? That time you threw a custard at Gertie Plumb and hit the works manager . . . and that time a man followed us all the way home and I dotted him one and it turned out to be your dad. Talk about laugh. . . . Well, it's something to look forward to, isn't it?

JOSIE. Fran . . .

FRAN. Yes, Josie?

JOSIE. I . . . I'm glad I knew you, Fran. . . .

FRAN. I'm glad I knew you, Josie. . . .

JOSIE. I'm glad.

Top Girls
Caryl Churchill

Marlene, a clever, able career woman, aged about 40, is the highly-successful managing director of Top Girls Employment Agency. One day her niece, Angie, aged 16, affectionate but 'simple', described as 'hopeless at school, lazy and disturbed . . . a victim of a competitive society', makes a surprise visit. Earlier in the play, Angie has said: 'I think I'm my aunt's child . . . I think my mum's really my aunt.' This is, in fact, true. The scene takes place in Marlene's office.
   Time: The present.

Main office. MARLENE *and* ANGIE. ANGIE *arrives.*

ANGIE. Hello.

MARLENE. Have you an appointment?

ANGIE. It's me. I've come.

MARLENE. What? It's not Angie?

ANGIE. It was hard to find this place. I got lost.

MARLENE. How did you get past the receptionist? The girl on the desk, didn't she try to stop you?

ANGIE. What desk?

MARLENE. Never mind.

ANGIE. I just walked in. I was looking for you.

MARLENE. Well you found me.

ANGIE. Yes.

MARLENE. So where's your mum? Are you up in town for the day?

ANGIE. Not really.

MARLENE. Sit down. Do you feel all right?

ANGIE. Yes thank you.

MARLENE. So where's Joyce?

ANGIE. She's at home.

MARLENE. Did you come up on a school trip then?

ANGIE. I've left school.

MARLENE. Did you come up with a friend?

ANGIE. No. There's just me.

MARLENE. You came up by yourself, that's fun. What have you been doing? Shopping? Tower of London?

ANGIE. No, I just come here. I come to you.

MARLENE. That's very nice of you to think of paying your aunty a visit. There's not many nieces make that the first port of call. Would you like a cup of coffee?

ANGIE. No thank you.

MARLENE. Tea, orange?

ANGIE. No thank you.

MARLENE. Do you feel all right?

ANGIE. Yes thank you.

MARLENE. Are you tired from the journey?

ANGIE. Yes, I'm tired from the journey.

MARLENE. You sit there for a bit then. How's Joyce?

ANGIE. She's all right.

28

MARLENE. Same as ever.

ANGIE. Oh yes.

MARLENE. Unfortunately you've picked a day when I'm rather busy, if there's ever a day when I'm not, or I'd take you out to lunch and we'd go to Madame Tussaud's. We could go shopping. What time do you have to be back? Have you got a day return?

ANGIE. No.

MARLENE. So what train are you going back on?

ANGIE. I came on the bus.

MARLENE. So what bus are you going back on? Are you staying the night?

ANGIE. Yes.

MARLENE. Who are you staying with? Do you want me to put you up for the night, is that it?

ANGIE. Yes please.

MARLENE. I haven't got a spare bed.

ANGIE. I can sleep on the floor.

MARLENE. You can sleep on the sofa.

ANGIE. Yes please.

MARLENE. I do think Joyce might have phoned me. It's like her.

ANGIE. This is where you work is it?

MARLENE. It's where I have been working the last two years but I'm going to move into another office.

ANGIE. It's lovely.

MARLENE. My new office is nicer than this. There's just the one big desk in it for me.

ANGIE. Can I see it?

MARLENE. Not now, no, there's someone else in it now. But he's leaving at the end of next week and I'm going to do his job.

ANGIE. Is that good?

MARLENE. Yes, it's very good.

ANGIE. Are you going to be in charge?

MARLENE. Yes I am.

ANGIE. I knew you would be.

MARLENE. How did you know?

ANGIE. I knew you'd be in charge of everything.

MARLENE. Not quite everything.

ANGIE. You will be.

MARLENE. Well we'll see.

ANGIE. Can I see it next week then?

MARLENE. Will you still be here next week?

ANGIE. Yes.

MARLENE. Don't you have to go home?

ANGIE. No.

MARLENE. Why not?

ANGIE. It's all right.

MARLENE. Is it all right?

ANGIE. Yes, don't worry about it.

MARLENE. Does Joyce know where you are?

ANGIE. Yes of course she does.

MARLENE. Well does she?

ANGIE. Don't worry about it.

MARLENE. How long are you planning to stay with me then?

ANGIE. You know when you came to see us last year?

MARLENE. Yes, that was nice wasn't it?

ANGIE. That was the best day of my whole life.

MARLENE. So how long are you planning to stay?

ANGIE. Don't you want me?

MARLENE. Yes yes, I just wondered.

ANGIE. I won't stay if you don't want me.

MARLENE. No, of course you can stay.

ANGIE. I'll sleep on the floor. I won't be any bother.

MARLENE. Don't get upset.

ANGIE. I'm not, I'm not. Don't worry about it.

Easy Virtue
Noel Coward

Marion, about 20, is 'largely made and pasty with lymphatic eyes . . .', her clothes 'slightly mannish'. She may one day be very handsome, but probably always rather bossy and opinionated. She disapproves of Larita, her brother's new wife, who is older than he, and also 'tall, exquisitely made up and very beautiful in simple, violently-expensive clothes.' The scene is in Marion's parents' country home.

Time: 1920s.

LARITA *is about to go upstairs when* MARION *comes down.*

MARION. Hallo! old girl.

LARITA. Hallo!

MARION. Are you going upstairs?

LARITA. I *was*. I thought of lying down a little.

MARION. You're always lying down.

LARITA. Yes, isn't it strange? I expect there's something organically wrong with me.

MARION (*anxiously*). I hope there isn't.

LARITA (*beginning to go*). Well, I'll see you later on –

MARION (*touching her arm*). Don't go. I've been wanting to talk to you.

LARITA. To me? Why – what about? – anything important?

MARION. No; just everything.

LARITA. That ought to take several years.

32

MARION (*laughing forcedly*). I didn't mean it literally.

LARITA. Oh, I see.

MARION. Have you got a cigarette on you?

LARITA. Yes, certainly. Here. (*She hands her case.*)

MARION (*taking one*). Thanks.

LARITA (*amiably*). Why aren't you watching the tennis?

MARION (*insensible of irony*). I've been too busy all the afternoon.

LARITA. How are all the preparations for to-night going?

MARION. All right. You're sitting next to Mr Furley.

LARITA. Splendid. Is he nice?

MARION. He's a damned good sort – rather High Church, you know; almost ritualistic.

LARITA. He won't be ritualistic at dinner, will he?

MARION. And you've got Sir George on the other side of you.

LARITA. Sir George who?

MARION. Sir George Bentley. He's awfully well up in dead languages and things.

LARITA. I do hope I shall be a comfort to him.

MARION. Very interesting man, George Bentley.

LARITA. How many are dining altogether?

MARION. Only twelve – we haven't really room for more comfortably.

LARITA. I hope it will all be an enormous success.

MARION. You won't be offended if I ask you something – just between ourselves?

LARITA. That depends, Marion. What is it?

MARION. Speaking as a pal, you know.

LARITA (*vaguely*). Oh yes – well?

MARION. Don't encourage father too much.

LARITA. In what way – encourage him? I don't understand.

MARION. Well, you know – you and he are always getting up arguments together.

LARITA. Why shouldn't we?

MARION. It annoys mother so when he tries to be funny.

LARITA. I've never noticed him trying to be funny – he's a very intelligent man.

MARION. Sometimes when you're discussing certain subjects, he says things which are not quite –

LARITA. You say 'certain subjects' in rather a sinister way, Marion. What subjects do you mean particularly?

MARION. Well, sex and things like that. You were talking about the Ericson divorce case the other day at lunch, when Harry Emsworth was here –

LARITA. It's an extraordinarily interesting case.

MARION. Yes, but one doesn't discuss things like that openly in front of strangers – I mean to say, it doesn't matter a bit when we're by ourselves; no one could be more broad-minded than I am – after all, what's the use of being in the world at all if you shut your eyes to things?

34

LARITA (*crisply*). Exactly.

MARION. You're not angry, are you?

LARITA. Angry? – no.

MARION. You see, I like you, Lari; we get on well together. I grant you we see things from different points of view, but that's only natural.

LARITA. Yes – oh yes.

MARION. I knew you'd be a sport about it and not mind. You see, my philosophy in life is frankness. Say what you've got to say, and have done.

LARITA. In other words – moral courage.

MARION. Yes, that's it.

LARITA. Why didn't you attack the Colonel on these little breaches of etiquette? He seems to be more to blame than I.

MARION. A woman always understands better than a man.

LARITA. Surely that's a little sweeping.

MARION. It's true, all the same. I knew you'd see.

LARITA. You weren't by any chance afraid that he'd laugh at you?

MARION. Good Heavens, no! I don't mind being laughed at.

LARITA. How extraordinary! I hate it.

MARION. What does it matter? If you've got something to say, say it.

LARITA. According to your code, the fact of having spoken like that about your father doesn't strike you as being disloyal in any way, does it?

MARION. Not between pals like us.

35

LARITA. Of course, yes – pals. I keep forgetting.

MARION. I believe you *are* angry.

LARITA. I'm not – but I'm very, very interested.

MARION. Look here, Lari, it's like this. Father's been a bit of a dog in his day. Mother's had a pretty bad time with him, and she's stood by him through thick and thin.

LARITA. How splendid!

MARION. Some men are like that – no moral responsibility. Edgar, you know, was just the same.

LARITA. You say 'was'. Has he reformed?

MARION. I think I've made him see – but it's been a tough struggle.

LARITA. What have you made him see?

MARION. I've made him see that nothing matters if you keep your life straight and decent.

LARITA. There are so many varying opinions as to what is straight and decent.

MARION. God admits of no varying opinions.

LARITA. Your religion must be wonderfully comforting. It makes you so sure of yourself.

MARION. If you're going to take up that tone, we won't discuss it.

LARITA. No – we'd better not.

MARION (*gently*). You mustn't jeer at religion, old girl. (*She puts her hand on her arm.*)

LARITA (*shaking her off*). I don't jeer at religion – but I jeer at hypocrisy.

MARION. *I'm* not a hypocrite – if that's what you mean.

LARITA (*quietly*). I'm afraid you are, Marion – and a disloyal one, too, which makes it all the more nauseating.

MARION. How dare you speak to me like that!

Kate and Emma
Monica Dickens

When Emma's magistrate father takes her to watch a Children's Court she first encounters Kate, then a difficult, unloved 16 year old, in care. Despite their very different backgrounds the two girls become friends, but Kate, though sensitive and intelligent and given the opportunity to change, becomes pregnant and marries while still in her teens. Now, a few years later, she lives with her four children in a room in a run-down London house. Unable to cope, ill, exhausted, Kate is huddled by a smoky fire when Emma arrives like a being from another world – well-dressed, in a good job, ready to help.

Time: The present.

EMMA (*offstage*). Hello . . . hello, Sammy . . . where's Mummy? . . . What's happened to your leg? Sammy? . . .

KATE. Who's that? Who is it, Sammy?

EMMA (*off*). It's me! (*She enters.*)

KATE. Hello, Em. (*She looks at her.*) I like your coat.

EMMA. Kate! (*She kisses her . . . looks around.*) Are you all right? The girls? . . . (*Over to the cot.*) The baby looks very pale. . . .

KATE. We're OK, Em . . . the girls have got colds . . . baby's fine . . . we'll all be good as new when spring comes . . . and when Bob gets home.

EMMA. Where is Bob?

KATE. In prison.

EMMA. Kate! Why didn't you tell me? I would have come

38

from anywhere. It must have been a nightmare. What did he do?

KATE. Tried to fix the gas meter. But he got caught.

EMMA. Oh, Kate . . . how awful for you!

KATE. Yeah . . . Oh, I don't know. I sometimes think I'm better off without him.

EMMA. He's like another child to take care of.

KATE. I didn't mind that. I could make him do what I wanted then, when he was babyish and silly. He still is, in a way, but in a different way. He's got violent, you know. He used to be such a gentle boy, but that's how getting to be a man has taken him.

EMMA. You mean he – he hits you?

KATE. Oh sure . . . (*Laughs.*) The things we used to think about marriage, they're not true, you know. Ask Sammy about his Dad.

EMMA. I saw Sammy outside, Kate . . . what on earth has he done to his leg?

KATE. He fell down. He's always falling down.

EMMA. I thought it looked like a burn. . . .

KATE. That's what I said. (*Quickly.*) He fell against the fire.

EMMA. Don't you keep the guard on?

KATE. Shut up lecturing and open that bottle of wine I can see in your bag.

(EMMA *pours out some wine, and hands a cup to* KATE. KATE, *after a few sips starts coughing harshly.*)

EMMA. Who's your doctor? I'm going to call him.

KATE. He won't come. They're so busy now, they'll only come to sign your death certificate.

EMMA. Then I'll take you to see him.

KATE. There's nothing wrong with me. It's over, what I had. It doesn't hurt now. Just a cigarette cough.

EMMA. I'm taking you to the doctor. (*Firmly.*) He can see the baby too. And Sammy's leg . . . (*She goes to window.*)

KATE. No, Em.

EMMA. Kate, it should be seen. . . . (*Looking out.*) Look at him, poor little chap. It's not healing. . . . Even I could see it's not a new burn. When did he do it?

KATE. Oh. . . . (*Looks away.*) I forget. . . . Some time ago.

EMMA. It's infected. You must take him.

KATE (*Looks* EMMA *straight in the eye*). I can't.

EMMA. Why not?

KATE. I can't trust him not to tell the doctor.

EMMA. Go on.

KATE. All right. I can't lie to you, Em. Why should I? It doesn't matter now. You've been here. If you don't come back, it's all one to me. (EMMA *doesn't reply*.) . . . I burned him with the poker. . . . It was when we last had the power cuts. The stove was right off, and I'd got the poker into the fire to heat a pan of water. He'd been a devil all day. It was when I was sick, I should have been in bed. I felt awful, but there was the baby, and Susannah was bilious, throwing up everywhere, and I was dragging about, and I couldn't stand no more. He messed his trousers – a child of four – and
40

before I knew what I was doing I'd caught him one across the back of the leg. All right? Now you know.

EMMA. The doctor needn't.

KATE. He'll know. The kid will tell him.

EMMA. He didn't tell me.

KATE. That's because I'm here. They'd get him in a room alone, and he'd tell. My mumma done that! Charming! They'd report me. That's what they do, you know. I heard Mrs Ellis say that to my mother once when I'd been shut in the yard all day. I'll report you, she said, but she didn't dare, with my dad the way he was. . . . Don't tell anyone, Em, please. You treat the burn. Get the proper stuff, you know what to do. It'll be all right if it's taken care of. I've just been feeling so rotten, I've let everything go. Now that you've come, it's going to be different. Don't spoil it, Em. Don't let me down. You swore, remember?

EMMA. I won't tell anyone, God help me. I'll get some burn dressing tomorrow, but if it gets worse . . .

KATE (*quickly*). Oh yes, of course, if it gets worse – I didn't mean it, Em. I'm not cruel, you know me. I did it in temper. I didn't know what I was doing.

EMMA. You'll have to watch yourself, Kate. If anything else happens it will be my fault now. You'll have to be more careful.

KATE. Don't preach at me. You don't know what it's like.

EMMA. It isn't the end of the world to have four children. Lots of women do. On purpose.

KATE. I don't care. It's different when you're poor all the time, and having no one to talk to – even when Bob's home. I can't help it if that kid gets on my nerves.

EMMA. There's nothing wrong with him. He's a darling boy.

KATE. He's got a devil in him.

EMMA. Don't talk like that. He's only a little child.

KATE. No one ever said I was only a little child when they –

EMMA. When what?

KATE. Nothing.

EMMA. If you were unhappy, all the more reason to see your children aren't.

KATE. You don't understand. You only have to be with kids once in a while – mine or anyone else's. You don't have to have them ALL the time. Every day. Every night. You feel lousy, and you want to stay in bed, and the baby cries and you get up to him, half-drugged with sleep, and then you sneak back for another half hour because you're so tired, so bloody tired. And just as you're going away into the only place where no-one can get at you – Waa-aa! It's another one starting up, and you've to begin all over again, and he hits her and she bites him, and they're all wet or hungry or sick or miserable and they all need you, so you may as well get up, and there's another day started.

EMMA. But if you lose your temper, they get worse, so what's it do?

KATE. Look, you don't plan to lose your temper. You just – you just – well, it's being so tired and fed up and there being no end to it. You've seen a fretsaw snap. Michael, Molly's oldest, he used to have one for his models, remember, with the pedals and that. One minute, buzzing along, eating the wood, spitting out the sawdust in a little cone on the rug. The next – ping! Up it flies in the air like a jack-knife – and I – I can't help it, Em. It's just I'm so bloody tired. . . . (*She cries, but after a while the cries turn to laughing. Then bitterly.*) Welcome back, Em, dear . . . I bet you're glad you came.

Middlemarch
George Eliot

Dorothea and Celia Brooke live with their Uncle at Tipton Grange in the provincial northern town of Middlemarch. Dorothea at 19 is a clever and rather serious young woman; Celia, younger, is both lighter-hearted and more worldly-wise. This conversation takes place at the beginning of the novel, in the drawing-room, after dinner.
   Time: 1870s.

CELIA. How very ugly Mr Casaubon is!

DOROTHEA. Celia! He is one of the most distinguished looking men I ever saw. He is remarkably like the portrait of Locke. He has the same deep eye sockets.

CELIA. Had Locke those two white moles with hairs on them?

DOROTHEA. Oh, I daresay! when people of a certain sort looked at him.

CELIA. Mr Casaubon is so sallow.

DOROTHEA. All the better. I suppose you admire a man with the complexion of a *cochon de lait*.

CELIA. Dodo! I never heard you make such a comparison before.

DOROTHEA. Why should I make it before the occasion came? It is a good comparison: the match is perfect.

CELIA. I wonder you show temper, Dorothea.

DOROTHEA. It is so painful in you, Celia, that you will
44

look at human beings as if they were merely animals with a toilette, and never see the great soul in a man's face.

CELIA (*a small hint of naïve malice*). Has Mr Casaubon a great soul?

DOROTHEA (*decisively*). Yes, I believe he has. Everything I see in him corresponds to his pamphlet on Biblical Cosmology.

CELIA. He talks very little.

DOROTHEA. There is no one for him to talk to.

CELIA. I suppose you quite despise Sir James Chettam?

DOROTHEA. No, he is a good creature, and more sensible than anyone would imagine.

CELIA. You mean that he appears silly.

DOROTHEA. No, no, but he does not talk equally well on all subjects.

CELIA. I should think none but disagreeable people do. They must be dreadful to live with. Only think! at breakfast and always.

DOROTHEA. Oh, Kitty, you are a wonderful creature! (*Laughing, pinching* CELIA's *chin in a fond way.*) Of course people need not be always talking well. Only one tells the quality of their minds when they try to talk well.

CELIA. You mean that Sir James tries and fails.

DOROTHEA. I was speaking generally. Why do you catechise me about Sir James? It is not the object of his life to please me.

CELIA. Now, Dodo, can you really believe that?

DOROTHEA. Certainly. He thinks of me as a future sister – that is all.

CELIA (*blushing*). Pray do not make that mistake any longer, Dodo. When Tantripp was brushing my hair the other day, she said that Sir James's man knew from Mrs Cadwallader's maid that Sir James was to marry the eldest Miss Brooke.

DOROTHEA (*indignantly*). How can you let Tantripp talk such gossip to you, Celia? You must have asked her questions. It is degrading.

CELIA. I see no harm at all in Tantripp's talking to me. It is better to hear what people say. You see what mistakes you make by taking up notions. I am quite sure that Sir James means to make you an offer: and he believes that you will accept him, especially since you have been so pleased with him about the plans you shall do for the cottages on his estate. And uncle too – I know he expects it. Everyone can see that Sir James is very much in love with you.

DOROTHEA. How could he expect it? I have never agreed with him about anything except the cottages: I was barely polite to him before.

CELIA. But you have been so pleased with him since then: he has begun to feel quite sure that you are fond of him.

DOROTHEA (*passionately*). Fond of him, Celia! How can you choose such odious expressions!?

CELIA. Dear me, Dorothea, I suppose it would be right for you to be fond of a man whom you accepted for a husband.

DOROTHEA. It is offensive to me to say that Sir James could think I was fond of him. Besides, it is not the right word for the feeling I must have towards the man I would accept as a husband.

46

CELIA. Well, I am sorry for Sir James. I thought it right to tell you, because you went on as you always do, never looking just where you are, and treading in the wrong place. You always see what nobody else sees; it is impossible to satisfy you: yet you never see what is quite plain. That's your way, Dodo.

DOROTHEA. It is very painful. I can have no more to do with his cottages. I must be uncivil to him. I must tell him I will have nothing to do with them. It is very painful.

CELIA. Wait a little. Think about it. You know he is going away for a day or two to see his sister. Poor Dodo . . . it is very hard: it is your favourite 'fad' to draw plans.

DOROTHEA. *Fad* to draw plans. Do you think I only care about my fellow creatures' houses in that childish way? I may well make mistakes. How can one ever do anything nobly Christian, living among people with such petty thoughts? . . . Celia, it is impossible that I should ever marry Sir James Chettam, and if he thinks of marrying me, he has made a great mistake.

Stamping, Shouting and Singing Home
Lisa Evans

Marguerite and her younger sister Lizzie are the great-great-grand-daughters of Sojourner Truth, once a slave, who fought tirelessly for the rights of black women. Lizzie, in her teens, narrates Sojourner's story, and also tells of what happens when Marguerite continues the struggle for black people. Before this scene between the girls, Mama has just told Lizzie, 'Beware of folk with their hearts eaten out.' Lizzie is a bright, lively girl; Marguerite already shows growing unease and anger. They are in their home in the American South.

Time: The present.

LIZZIE *climbs off the stool and starts to unpick the old seams of the garment* MAMA *pinned.*

LIZZIE. Now there's several ways to eat out the heart. Take the movies. Me, I used to save up pennies and go every chance I had. Hollywood, California, Sunset Strip – these were powerful magical words conjuring up for me how the world outside our town was. I told Marguerite about it when I got home. She was still out of a job and had taken to going out alone all of a sudden and coming back with bundles hid under her sweater. She was getting awful secretive and if there's one thing I can't abide it's secrets.

Scene Six. LIZZIE *is practising tap dancing like the movies.*

LIZZIE. Hi Marguerite.

MARGUERITE. Hi.

LIZZIE. You been someplace nice?

MARGUERITE. Mn.

48

LIZZIE. Sky fell in just afore dinnertime.

MARGUERITE. Oh yea.

LIZZIE. Thirty people injured by falling stars.

MARGUERITE. Really.

LIZZIE. It's like talking to Adam. I'm not keen on snakes though so I keep on trying. What you got under your sweater Marguerite?

MARGUERITE. Nothing.

LIZZIE. Well in that case if I was you I'd get on down see the doctor real fast cos you got a bump developing in the wrong place, sister.

MARGUERITE. That so? (MARGUERITE *opens the tin trunk, slithers something inside and locks it again.*)

LIZZIE. Hey Marguerite, where d'you find a turtle with no legs?

MARGUERITE. I don't know.

LIZZIE. Where you left it. (*No response.*) Where you left it, get it? You know Marguerite, I saw this movie and I reckon I know why you can't get a job. See, all the black folks in the movies who wait on table, are housemaids and all, well even in the old days, they smile. And when they ain't waiting on tables smiling, they dancing and smiling. They never stop smiling. Like they advertising toothpaste dawn to dusk. Don't known how they eat their food wearing those big grins – but they don't show you that part. Must be kinda difficult. But if you practised in front of the mirror I'm sure you could learn it.

MARGUERITE. What!

LIZZIE. I should have seen the weather signs but I just ploughed on in. Today I saw this one about Al Jolson. He

49

sings our songs and there was this one Mama would have liked real well – all about his mother. (LIZZIE *tap dances and sings, minstrel-style: 'Mammee'. She is really enjoying herself.*)

MARGUERITE. Shut up.

LIZZIE. And there was me thinking I had a future in show business.

MARGUERITE. Don't you ever sing that song.

LIZZIE. What's the matter with you?

MARGUERITE. You ever hear your mother called 'Mammee?'

LIZZIE. No but . . .

MARGUERITE. You ever heard any black folks singing that song?

LIZZIE. Well no, but . . .

MARGUERITE. 'Swannee River'?

LIZZIE. You seen the movie! Why didn't you say so?

MARGUERITE. I seen some white guy blacking his face, making up songs about the brothers and sisters. What he know about being black? He's just making money off of our backs.

LIZZIE. It's only a movie.

MARGUERITE. And the way they tell it, you only some happy grinning nigger!

LIZZIE. Come to think on it, not only did I not know one woman answering to the name of 'Mammee', but I couldn't recall anyone I'd met smiling that much neither –
50

particularly when they cleaning up someone else's mess. Marguerite?

MARGUERITE. Yes.

LIZZIE. Do they have a lot of black folks in Hollywood, you know, like producers and directors and all?

MARGUERITE. What do you think, dummy?

LIZZIE (*to the audience*). Dummy huh? When they make us look foolish it's to keep us under and make them look smart, right?

MARGUERITE. Right.

LIZZIE. They shouldn't do that, should they?

MARGUERITE. No, they shouldn't.

LIZZIE. And the only way we can find out and tell it like it is, is to ask, right?

MARGUERITE. Of course.

LIZZIE. And brothers and sisters should be treated with respect.

MARGUERITE. That's right, yes.

LIZZIE. In that case I don't think you ought to call me dummy, and what you got in that box?

MARGUERITE. Corpses.

LIZZIE. What?

MARGUERITE. Corpses.

LIZZIE. Real live corpses?

MARGUERITE. Corpses. (MARGUERITE *exits*.)

LIZZIE. Well, I just contemplating whether to have one of the fainting fits I hear tell white folks so good at. Perhaps my sister taken to murdering awful small people. I feel the spring coiling tighter and all of a sudden I could hear the dogs of evil snapping at our heels, they slipped their chains and running lose. Somebody going to get bit. Top it all, Mama comes in yelling . . .

[MAMA (*offstage*) You forgot to feed the chickens!]

(*Song: 'Hush You Bye', hummed through this next speech and then sung at the end.*)

LIZZIE. And it wasn't even my turn! Outside I made toe patterns in the dust, wondering why I'm always the one getting hollered at. Stayed out there, thinking about running away, till the mockingbird stopped calling, dark was wrapping all around me, and it didn't seem like such a good idea. Maybe I'd go some other time instead.

Walking Through Seaweed
Ian Hamilton Finlay

This is a shortened version of a one-act two-hander. Two teenage girls are in a city street at dusk. They have sauntered up to look in a shop window. Three doors away is a cafe with a juke-box, its raucous or wistful pop songs carrying faintly into the street. The setting could be anywhere in England.

Time: The 1960s.

FIRST GIRL See them toffee apples in the window?

SECOND GIRL. Yep.

FIRST GIRL. Real old-fashioned they look. . . . Fancy toffee apples . . .

SECOND GIRL. You ever ate toffee apples?

FIRST GIRL. Yep. Sure we ate them. Lots of times. When I was wee we was great on toffee apples. But I wouldn't eat one now. It'd be undignified.

SECOND GIRL. Maybe I could go in the shop and get one of them toffee apples. . . .

FIRST GIRL. And eat it now . . . out here in the street? Not when you're out with me you don't eat a toffee apple. . . .

SECOND GIRL. Oh well, all right . . . But I think it would be nice to have eaten one of them toffee apples.

FIRST GIRL. It's all right for kids to eat toffee apples. But we ain't kids now. We're sixteen.

53

SECOND GIRL. Yep. Grown-up women. (*Pause. The pop music grows momentarily louder.*) How do you like that one that's on the juke-box in the cafe now?

FIRST GIRL. I never heard that one before.

SECOND GIRL. It was on the telly.

FIRST GIRL. We ain't got a telly yet.

SECOND GIRL. No.

FIRST GIRL. Everyone around us . . . they've all got tellys. . . .

SECOND GIRL. Yep. . . . Them toffee apples look real good. . . . And d'you see them liquorice straps?

FIRST GIRL. Which?

SECOND GIRL. There – by the sweetie cigarettes. You see them?

FIRST GIRL. Yep. We ate them too.

SECOND GIRL. You know what I always think of when I see those old-fashioned rolled-up liquorice straps?

FIRST GIRL. No.

SECOND GIRL. Seaweed

FIRST GIRL. What?

SECOND GIRL. Seaweed. (*Pause.*) You ever walked through seaweed? – that seaweed that grows by the sea . . . you know? That seaweed that's all slippery . . . and mostly brown . . . like them straps of liquorice?

FIRST GIRL. No.

SECOND GIRL. You never took your shoes and stockings off and sort of – paddled through it?

FIRST GIRL. No. I'd be scared to.

54

SECOND GIRL. Why'd you be scared to?

FIRST GIRL. Maybe there'd be crabs in it would come and bite you – and – and I'd be scared to walk through seaweed.

SECOND GIRL. Oh, but it's lovely to walk in seaweed. . . . You take off your shoes and your socks – and you carry them . . . and you go walking all through it . . . right up to your ankles in it – like a dancer . . . it makes you feel like a dancer . . .

FIRST GIRL. I like dancing . . .

SECOND GIRL. So do I.

FIRST GIRL. I like rock and roll . . . and jiving . . .

SECOND GIRL. I like that too . . . it's lovely.

FIRST GIRL. Everyone goes jiving.

SECOND GIRL. Yep . . . (*Pause.*) You got a boy-friend?

FIRST GIRL. Yep. I got lots of them.

SECOND GIRL. You got lots of boy-friends?

FIRST GIRL. Yep.

SECOND GIRL. What d'you do with them?

FIRST GIRL. Not much. . . . Go jiving.

SECOND GIRL. That all?

FIRST GIRL. Go to the pictures.

SECOND GIRL. That all?

FIRST GIRL. What else? – Go jiving, go to the pictures. Play the juke-box in a cafe. What else?

SECOND GIRL. I got a boy-friend.

FIRST GIRL. Have you?

SECOND GIRL. Yep. I got a boy-friend. And he's sort of special. I mean – I mean I've just the one special boy-friend – and d'you know what he and I do?

FIRST GIRL. Go to the pictures?

SECOND GIRL. No.

FIRST GIRL. Go jiving?

SECOND GIRL. No.

FIRST GIRL. Well, what d'you do? You'll have to tell me.

SECOND GIRL. Me and my boy-friend – I told you he's special – *we* go WALKING THROUGH SEAWEED.

FIRST GIRL. You don't!

SECOND GIRL. But we do . . . we go . . . in his car . . . down to where the sea is, and then we take off our shoes . . . and we walk through the seaweed . . . it's ever so lovely!

FIRST GIRL. You must be crackers, you and your boy-friend.

SECOND GIRL. We are not crackers. He's a very nice boy (*Pause.*) And while we're walking along through the sea-weed . . . he's ever such a nice boy . . . he takes hold of my hand . . .

FIRST GIRL. What does he do?

SECOND GIRL. When we're walking?

FIRST GIRL. No, what does he DO? What does he work at?

SECOND GIRL. He's in advertising.

FIRST GIRL. What's his name?

SECOND GIRL. His first name's Paul.

FIRST GIRL. You aren't just making all this up are you?

SECOND GIRL. How'd I be making it up? I told you his name didn't I? His name's Paul and he's ever so handsome . . . he has nice dark hair and he's kind of smooth . . .

FIRST GIRL. It doesn't sound to me like a nice, smooth, handsome boy that's in advertising – a kind of boy like this Paul – would want to go walking through a lot of seaweed.

SECOND GIRL. I beg your pardon but he does. Let me tell you he wouldn't *mind* getting bitten by a crab. (*Pause.*) The fact is, he's *fond* of crabs.

FIRST GIRL. How come you happen to meet this Paul fellow who's so handsome and works in advertising?

SECOND GIRL. We met at a dance.

FIRST GIRL. I never met any handsome smooth fellows – out of advertising – at a dance. . . .

SECOND GIRL. Well, maybe you will. . . .

FIRST GIRL. I *read* of them in magazines . . . I read of *lots* of them in that magazine my Mum gets . . . Tall, dark and smooth . . . And come to think of it *their* name was Paul.

SECOND GIRL. Paul is a very common name in advertising. What's the name of *your* boy-friend?

FIRST GIRL. I already told you, I got lots of boy-friends. I can't remember their names off-hand. What does Paul do in that advertising place?

SECOND GIRL. Well . . . what he does . . . is . . . is go to conferences.

FIRST GIRL. I read about them conferences in my Mum's magazine. There's this boy . . . the one called Paul, you know . . . the one who's sort of smooth and dark and handsome – and what he does is . . . go to conferences.

SECOND GIRL. Like Paul. Paul goes to conferences.

FIRST GIRL. What about the other one?

SECOND GIRL. I ain't *got* another one.

FIRST GIRL. Come off it . . . What about the one with ginger hair and a snub nose. The engineer.

SECOND GIRL. I don't know any engineers.

FIRST GIRL. I bet *he* wouldn't walk through seaweed. I bet the ginger one with the snub nose spends *his* Saturdays at a football match.

SECOND GIRL. I don't love *him*. I love Paul.

FIRST GIRL. One of these days – you and Paul – you're going to be sorry for walking through seaweed.

SECOND GIRL. Why?

FIRST GIRL. You're going to get bit . . . that's why.

SECOND GIRL. We *never* get bit. . . . But we just *might* though. That's what's so nice about walking through seaweed . . . that you might get bit . . . just a *little* . . . and when we've walked all through the seaweed . . .

FIRST GIRL. Seaweed ain't nice . . . and the sea ain't nice . . . and having no telly ain't. . . . Eating toffee apples ain't nice either. I wouldn't put a toe in that seaweed.

SECOND GIRL. But it's beautiful the sea. . . . Did you ever dream of it?

FIRST GIRL. I don't have dreams . . . only once I dreamed we had a telly . . . a great big telly, yards across . . .

SECOND GIRL. I dreamed of the sea once . . . it was all big and . . . dark . . . well . . . it was – beautiful!

58

FIRST GIRL. It was hi-fi stereoscopic with five extra loudspeakers. . . .

SECOND GIRL. Maybe you could come down with us to the sea . . . I could hold your hand – like Paul holds my hand. . . .

FIRST GIRL. You ain't like a magazine fellow that would make me feel all right about that seaweed. . . .

SECOND GIRL. I'd hold it tight . . . ever so tight . . . we could go walking . . . like dancers . . . you and me . . . we could walk through the seaweed . . . all the way . . . right to the sea. . . . And seaweed . . . it's full of crabs and things . . . but you got to walk through it . . . because it's lovely . . . you got to walk – like a dance . . . all through the seaweed . . . right to the sea!

FIRST GIRL. All my life I kept out of seaweed. I stayed away from seaweed. It ain't . . . well, nice stuff. You can go and walk in all that seaweed . . . you can go if you want to – but not with *me*!

SECOND GIRL. I like the look of them toffee apples . . .

FIRST GIRL. They're just for kids. (*Pause.*) Let's go in the cafe now . . . I like that one that's on the juke-box . . . though it's kind of sad . . . Come on . . . let's go.

SECOND GIRL. Yep. Let's go in the cafe and play the juke-box. . . .

The Virtuous Burglar
Dario Fo (translated by Jo Farrell)

The opening scene of a one-act Italian farce based on a hilarious confusion of identities. . . . Actors are free to make their own decisions as to the ages and types of the characters.

Time: written in the 1950s, but could be set earlier or later this century.

A BURGLAR, *having forced open a window, is climbing into a third floor apartment in a well-to-do block of flats. On one side stands a classical shaded lamp. He looks around carefully. From the dark, we see furniture, rugs, old valuable paintings emerge. The* BURGLAR *closes the shutters, then switches on the light.*

Just when he is about to pull open a drawer, the telephone rings. His first panic-stricken impulse is to make off as quickly as possible but then, realising that no one in the house comes to answer it and that he has nothing to fear, he returns to where he was. He would like to ignore the ringing of the phone but cannot. He makes his way stealthily over to the phone and leaps at it. He grabs the receiver and, almost as if he wished to suffocate it, presses it against his chest, covering it with his jacket. As though to make the act seem more criminal, an increasingly feeble and suffocated sound begins to emerge from the receiver.

BURGLAR'S WIFE. Hello. Hello. Would you kindly answer. . . . Who's speaking?

(The BURGLAR *can finally let out a sigh of relief. The voice has stopped. The* BURGLAR *takes the receiver from under his jacket, raises it cautiously and puts it to his ear. Then he shakes it several times and hears a kind of groan.)*

60

BURGLAR. Oh! At last.

BURGLAR'S WIFE. Ooooh! At last . . . who's speaking?

BURGLAR (*surprised once again*). Maria. Is that you?

BURGLAR'S WIFE. Yes, it's me. Why didn't you reply?

(*At this point, lit up by one of the footlights, the figure of the woman who is speaking on the phone appears on the side of the stage which has so far remained in darkness.*)

BURGLAR. You're crazy! Are you even phoning me at work now? Suppose there had been someone in the house? You're a great help you are.

BURGLAR'S WIFE. But you told me yourself that the owners were at their country cottage . . . anyway, I'm sorry, but I just couldn't stand it any more . . . I was worried about you . . . I didn't feel well . . . even a few moments ago, when I was ringing up, I could hardly breathe.

BURGLAR. Oh well, I'm sorry too, I didn't mean it, it never occurred to me that it might be you . . .

BURGLAR'S WIFE. And just what do you mean by that?

BURGLAR. Nothing, nothing . . . but let me get on . . . I've already wasted enough time.

BURGLAR'S WIFE. Ah, I'm wasting your time now! Thank you very much. Here I am in agony, nearly sick with worry . . . I don't know what to do with myself . . .

BURGLAR. What are you doing?

BURGLAR'S WIFE. I'm going through absolute hell, all because of you . . . and you treat me like this . . . charming, just charming that is . . . but don't worry . . . from now on I'm not interested . . . from now on don't even bother telling me where you're going, because as far as I am concerned . . .

61

BURGLAR. My dear, try and be reasonable . . . Can't you get it into your sweet head that I am not here for fun . . . just this once, couldn't you let me get on with my burgling in peace?

BURGLAR'S WIFE. There you go. You're at it again. Playing the martyr. There are plenty of people who burgle, shoplift, even go in for armed robbery without all this fuss. Just as well you stick to petty crime, otherwise God knows what sort of state I'd be in.

BURGLAR (*who has heard a strange noise behind him, instinctively putting his hand over the mouthpiece*). Quiet! (*Fortunately it was only the sound of the grandfather clock about to strike. It strikes midnight.*)

BURGLAR'S WIFE. What's that?

BURGLAR (*recovering from his fright*). It's only the grandfather clock, thank goodness.

BURGLAR'S WIFE. What a clear sound it has! – It must be quite old. Is it very heavy?

BURGLAR (*absent-mindedly*). Might be quite . . . (*Suddenly realizing his wife's intentions.*) Come on . . . You're not really expecting me to bring it home . . . sometimes I wonder . . .

BURGLAR'S WIFE. Oh no, don't you bother your little head about me . . . How could you imagine that I'd ask anything like that . . . a nice thought from you! . . . You giving a little present to me! . . . The very idea!

BURGLAR. You're mad, that's what you are . . . If I try to carry off that box, you tell me where to put the silverware and anything else I find.

BURGLAR'S WIFE. In the box . . .

62

BURGLAR (*sarcastically*). You wouldn't like me to bring home a fridge? There's a nice big one through there, with a freezer department.

BURGLAR'S WIFE. Don't raise your voice, please. You're not at home now.

BURGLAR. Sorry. I got carried away.

BURGLAR'S WIFE. Besides, you might be overheard, and you'd look singularly ill-mannered.

BURGLAR. I've already said I'm sorry.

BURGLAR'S WIFE. And anyway, I didn't say I wanted a fridge, never mind one with a freezer compartment, I wouldn't know where to put it. But I would like a little something . . . it's the thought that counts. I'll leave it to you. It's you that's giving the present, after all.

BURGLAR. How am I supposed to know what you would like. I've got other things on my mind right now.

BURGLAR'S WIFE. If that's all it is, I could come along and choose it myself.

BURGLAR. That's all I'd need!

BURGLAR'S WIFE. I'd love to see what a real luxury flat is like. I'd make them die with envy at the coffee morning.

BURGLAR. It's me that'll die from something or other, not the women at the coffee morning . . . I'm here to burgle this house, can you not understand that? Cheerio, see you later.

BURGLAR'S WIFE. What's the rush? Is it too much for you to be nice to me once in a while? I am your wife after all. You even married me in church, not in a registry, like some whore, so you can't get out of it.

BURGLAR (*annoyed*). I've already said goodbye.

BURGLAR'S WIFE. Just a little kiss.

BURGLAR. Oh all right. (*He purses his lips in a comic way and emits a loud kissing sound.*)

BURGLAR'S WIFE. Do you love me?

BURGLAR. Yes I love you.

BURGLAR'S WIFE. Very much?

BURGLAR (*at the end of his tether*). Very, very much. But now will you put down the phone?

BURGLAR'S WIFE. You first.

BURGLAR. All right . . . me first. (*He is about to put the phone down when he hears his wife's voice assailing him loudly for the last time.*)

BURGLAR'S WIFE. Don't forget the present! (*The BURGLAR replaces the phone, staring at it all the while with hatred. At that moment the figure of the woman disappears in the dark. Finally alone, the BURGLAR begins to look around the apartment in search of his booty.*)

'Tis Pity She's a Whore
John Ford

*An Elizabethan play, set as was fashionable at the time, in Italy.
Annabella and Giovanni are the son and daughter of a nobleman,
Florio. Both are attractive and clever; he renowned for his academic
scholarship, her hand sought by rivalling suitors. In this scene they
confess their deep love for each other. They are in the hall of Florio's
house.*

  Time: 1633.

Enter GIOVANNI.

GIOVANNI. Lost! I am lost! my fates have doomed my
death:
The more I strive, I love; the more I love,
The less I hope: I see my ruin certain.
What judgment or endeavours could apply
To my incurable and restless wounds,
I thoroughly have examined, but in vain.
O, that it were not in religion sin
To make our love a god, and worship it!
I have even wearied Heaven with prayers, dried up
The spring of my continual tears, even starved
My veins with daily fasts: what wit or art
Could counsel, I have practised; but, alas,
I find all these but dreams, and old men's tales,
To fright unsteady youth; I'm still the same:
Or I must speak, or burst. 'Tis not, I know,
My lust, but 'tis my fate that leads me on.
Keep fear and low faint-hearted shame with slaves!
I'll tell her that I love her, though my heart

Were rated at the price of that attempt. –
O me! she comes.

Enter ANNABELLA.

ANNABELLA.　　　　Brother!
GIOVANNI (*aside*).　　　　　　　　If such a thing
As courage dwell in men, ye heavenly powers,
Now double all that virtue in my tongue!

ANNABELLA. Why, brother.
Will you not speak to me?

GIOVANNI.　　　　　　　Yes: how d'ye, sister?

ANNABELLA. Howe'er I am, methinks you are not well.

GIOVANNI. Come, sister, lend your hand: let's walk
together!
I hope you need not blush to walk with me;
Here's none but you and I.

ANNABELLA.　　　　　　How's this?

GIOVANNI.　　　　　　　　　I'faith,
I mean no harm.

ANNABELLA.　　　Harm?

GIOVANNI.　　　　　　　No, good faith.
How is't with ye?

ANNABELLA (*aside*).　　　I trust he be not frantic.
I am very well, brother.

GIOVANNI. Trust me, but I am sick; I fear so sick
'Twill cost my life.

ANNABELLA. Mercy forbid it! 'tis not so, I hope.

GIOVANNI. I think you love me, sister.
66

ANNABELLA. Yes, you know
I do.

GIOVANNI. I know't, indeed. – You're very fair.

ANNABELLA. Nay, then I see you have a merry sickness.

GIOVANNI. That's as it proves. The poets feign, I read,
That Juno for her forehead did exceed
All other goddesses; but I durst swear
Your forehead exceeds hers, as hers did theirs.

ANNABELLA. 'Troth, this is pretty!

GIOVANNI. Such a pair of stars
As are thine eyes would, like Promethean fire,
If gently glanced, give life to senseless stones.

ANNABELLA. Fie upon ye!

GIOVANNI. The lily and the rose, most sweetly strange,
Upon your dimpled cheeks do strive for change:
Such lips would tempt a saint; such hands as those
Would make an anchorite lascivious.

ANNABELLA. D'ye mock me or flatter me?

GIOVANNI. If you would see a beauty more exact
Than art can counterfeit or nature frame,
Look in your glass, and there behold your own.

ANNABELLA. O, you are a trim youth!

GIOVANNI. Here! (*Offers his dagger to her.*)

ANNABELLA. What to do?

GIOVANNI. And here's my breast; strike home!
Rip up my bosom; there thou shalt behold
A heart in which is writ the truth I speak.
Why stand ye?

67

ANNABELLA.   Are you earnest?

GIOVANNI.   Yes, most earnest.
You cannot love?

ANNABELLA.   Whom?

GIOVANNI.   Me.   My tortured soul
Hath felt affliction in the heat of death.
O, Annabella, I am quite undone!
The love of thee, my sister, and the view
Of thy immortal beauty have untuned
All harmony both of my rest and life.
Why d'ye not strike?

ANNABELLA.   Forbid it, my just fears!
If this be true, 'twere fitter I were dead.

GIOVANNI. True, Annabella! 'tis no time to jest.
I have too long suppressed the hidden flames
That almost have consumed me: I have spent
Many a silent night in sighs and groans;
Ran over all my thoughts, despised my fate,
Reasoned against the reasons of my love,
Done all that smoothed-cheeked virtue could advise;
But found all bootless: 'tis my destiny
That you must either love, or I must die.

ANNABELLA. Comes this in sadness[1] from you?

GIOVANNI.   Let some mischief
Befall me soon, if I dissemble aught.

ANNABELLA. You are my brother Giovanni.

GIOVANNI.   You
My sister Annabella; I know this,
And could afford you instance why to love

1. *earnest*

So much the more for this; to which intent
Wise nature first in your creation meant
To make you mine; else't had been sin and foul
To share one beauty to a double soul.
Nearness in birth and blood doth but persuade
A nearer nearness in affection.
I have asked counsel of the holy church,
Who tells me I may love you; and 'tis just
That, since I may, I should; and will, yes, will.
Must I now live or die?

ANNABELLA.   Live; thou hast won
The field, and never fought: what thou hast urged
My captive heart had long ago resolved.
I blush to tell thee, – but I'll tell thee now, –
For every sigh that thou hast spent for me
I have sighed ten; for every tear shed twenty:
And not so much for that I loved, as that
I durst not say I loved, nor scarcely think it.

GIOVANNI. Let not this music be a dream, ye gods,
For pity's sake, I beg ye!

ANNABELLA.   On my knees,   (*She kneels.*)
Brother, even by our mother's dust, I charge you,
Do not betray me to your mirth or hate:
Love me or kill me, brother.

GIOVANNI.   On my knees,   (*He kneels.*)
Sister, even by my mother's dust, I charge you,
Do not betray me to your mirth or hate:
Love me or kill me, sister.

ANNABELLA. You mean good sooth, then?

GIOVANNI.   In good troth, I do;
And so do you, I hope: say, I'm in earnest.

ANNABELLA. I'll swear it, I.

GIOVANNI. And I; and by this kiss – (*Kisses her.*)
Once more, yet once more: now let's rise, – by this,
I would not change this minute for Elysium.
What must we now do?

ANNABELLA. What you will.

GIOVANNI. Come, then;
After so many tears as we have wept,
Let's learn to court in smiles, to kiss, and sleep. (*Exeunt.*)

Alphabetical Order
Michael Frayn

Leslie, in her mid-twenties, is a mixture of shyness and assertiveness, with a driving sense of organisation, somewhat alarming to her colleagues on the library staff of a provincial newspaper. Although the 'new girl,' she has reorganised the place completely, while still attempting to keep on the right side of Lucy, who is about 35, very popular, easy-going and dreadfully unorganised.

Time: 1975.

LUCY *enters in haste, wearing the fur coat she bought and clutching a supermarket carrier-bag full of groceries*

LUCY. Sorry. There was only one checkout working. Hello, John. Sorry, Leslie.

LESLIE. You're not late.

LUCY (*dumping the groceries on her desk*). I couldn't shop this morning because I was listening out for the baby downstairs.

LESLIE. I've only just got here myself.

LUCY (*pulling the groceries out of the bag until she finds an apple to eat*). If she takes the baby she has to take the pram, and if she takes the pram she can't get on the bus, and if she can't get on the bus she arrives too late for the doctor to see the baby. Of course, if she leaves the baby the doctor doesn't see him either, but at least she has time to do some shopping. Sorry. (*She dumps her coat on top of the groceries.*)

LESLIE. Wouldn't you be happier if we hung that up?

LUCY. Oh, sorry. (*She picks it up.* LESLIE *politely takes it from her and hangs it up.*) Sorry. What do you want me to do today? (*She puts the apple into the drawer of her desk.*)

LESLIE. What do you think we should be doing today?

LUCY. I hope you're just about to tell me.

LESLIE. Well, I was wondering if you might like to get on with marking up and cutting.

LUCY. Sure.

LESLIE. Because I was wondering if you might like me to do some more discarding.

LUCY. Anything you say.

LESLIE. We've still got a lot of dead wood to get rid of.

LUCY. Right. Where are the papers? (*She crosses to Leslie's table.*)

LESLIE. I was wondering do you think it would be a good idea if I got started on the old Balance of Payments folders? (*She hands her the day's papers.*)

LUCY. You've *got* started on them.

LESLIE. Just while I was waiting.

LUCY. I *am* late.

LESLIE. You're *not* late.

LUCY. Sorry.

LESLIE. I was early.

LUCY. Oh. Sorry, anyway. (*The telephone rings.* LESLIE *looks at her watch, then picks up the telephone.*)

LESLIE (*into the telephone*). Library . . . (*Into the telephone.*) In gross tons or short tons? (LUCY *sits down at her table and* *spreads out the first of the papers on top of the junk. Into the telephone.*) One-two-nine, seven-six-nine, five-o-o. One-six-o, three-nine-one, five-o-four. Two-two-seven, four-eight-nine, eight-six-four. . . . All right? . . . Not at all. (*She puts the telephone down.*)

LUCY. Work-to-Rule Brings Chaos to Midlands. Storm of Protests Over PM on TV . . . Oh God. I hate this job. I hate this place.

LESLIE. Would you be happier working at my table?

LUCY. No.

LESLIE. I'm only discarding. I can work on top of the filing-cabinets.

LUCY. Don't *you* hate it?

LESLIE. Come on, you sit here.

LUCY. I don't want to sit there. Don't you hate this work?

LESLIE. Yes.

LUCY. Do you?

LESLIE. Of course I hate it.

LUCY (*thinking about this*). No, you don't. You love it.

LESLIE. I'm dependent on it. That's what I hate.

LUCY. You're a natural for it. You've got an instinct for order.

LESLIE. It's a compulsion. I hate the feeling of being compelled.

LUCY. You're as happy as a child making mud pies.

LESLIE. I hate the mud.

LUCY. Well, mud pies are an improvement on mud.

LESLIE. Mud pies are mud. And mud's mud. (*Silence.*)

73

LUCY (*cutting*). Middle East Dominates Ottawa Talks. Second Congo Fears Sway UN Vote . . . (*She sings.*) Mud, mud, glorious mud! Nothing quite like it for cooling the blood.

LESLIE. You did think we should discard everything in the old Balance of Payments folders except the raw monthly figures, didn't you?

LUCY. *I* thought so?

LESLIE. I *think* you did.

LUCY. *You* thought so.

LESLIE. I think we did talk about it.

LUCY. I think you wondered whether I thought it would be a good idea.

LESLIE. I think you thought it would.

LUCY. I think I thought whatever you thought. (*Pause.*)

LESLIE. I don't want to do it if you *don't* think it's a good idea.

LUCY. No. (*She laughs.*)

LESLIE. What?

LUCY. Yes! I *do* think it's a good idea! (*Pause.*)

LESLIE. Look, all I can do is to make suggestions.

LUCY. That's right.

LESLIE. It's up to you to say whether you think they're a good idea or not.

LUCY. Of course it is. And I do.

LESLIE. You do what?

LUCY. Think they're a good idea. Nuclear power stations. What are we filing them under these days? Atomic Energy Authority, or Central Electricity Generating Board?

LESLIE. Nuclear power stations? We file them under Nuclear Power Stations.

LUCY. Oh. Well, that's one way of doing it.

LESLIE. Unless you'd like to go back to the old system?

LUCY. That's right. We'll go back to the old system. (LESLIE *looks at her. She says nothing.*) I said, we'll go back to the old system. Whatever that was.

LESLIE. Look, if you want to, you've only got to say.

LUCY. I've said.

LESLIE. No, seriously.

LUCY. Seriously. (LESLIE *looks at her.* LUCY *laughs.*) Sorry.

LESLIE. All right, we'll move the tables back together again.

LUCY. The tables?

LESLIE. Isn't it the tables you're worrying about?

LUCY. I'm not worrying about anything.

LESLIE. It is the tables, isn't it?

LUCY. No.

LESLIE. It was just an idea, putting them round this way.

LUCY. It's a good idea.

LESLIE. I thought you thought you'd be happier if your stuff wasn't spreading over on to my table all the time?

LUCY. Is that what I thought?

LESLIE. I *thought* that's what you thought. (*Pause.*)

LUCY. I love looking at this bit of wall.

LESLIE. Look, if you *want* to move the tables back . . .

LUCY. No, no, no, no. (*Pause.*)

LESLIE. It's this place that's getting us down.

LUCY. That's right.

LESLIE. It'll be better when we've got things straight.

LUCY. Haven't we got things straight?

LESLIE. We haven't finished getting them straight.

LUCY. No, that'll be the day. When we've finished getting things straight. When we've got everything finally and permanently straight.

My Children, My Africa
Athol Fugard

*An interschool debate is taking place in a South African country town
and Isabel, a girl from a white school, and Thami, a boy from a black
school, both about 18, are being coached by the latter's teacher, Mr M.
The friction between Thami and Mr M is linked to the political
situation in the country. Thami remains tense and unyielding in his
views, unable to accept Isabel's more relaxed and open outlook.*
   Time: 1980s.

ISABEL. (*sensitive to a change of mood in* THAMI). I think
you'll like my folks. My Mom's a bit on the reserved side but
that's just because she's basically very shy. But you and my
Dad should get on well. Start talking sport with him and he
won't let you go. He played cricket for EP, you know.
(*Pause.*) You will come, won't you?

THAMI (*edge to his voice*). Didn't you hear Mr M? 'A
delight and a privilege! We accept most gratefully.' (*Writing
in his notebook.*) Charles Dickens . . . Thomas Hardy . . .
Jane Austen . . .

ISABEL. Was he speaking for you as well?

THAMI. He speaks for me on nothing!

ISABEL. Relax . . . I know that. That's why I tried to ask
you separately and why I'll ask you again. Would you like to
come to tea next Sunday to meet my family? It's not a polite
invitation. They really want to meet you.

THAMI. Me? Why? Are they starting to get nervous?

ISABEL. Oh, come off it, Thami. Don't be like that.
They're always nervous when it comes to me. But this time it

77

happens to be genuine interest. I've told you. I talk about you at home. They know I have a good time with you . . . that we're a team . . . which they are now very proud of, incidentally . . . and that we're cramming like lunatics so that we can put up a good show at the festival. Is it so strange that they want to meet you after all that? Honestly, sometimes dealing with the two of you is like walking on a tightrope. I'm always scared I'm going to put a foot wrong and . . . well I just *hate* being scared like that. (*A few seconds of truculent silence between the two of them.*) What's going on, Thami? Between you two? There's something very wrong, isn't there?

THAMI. No more than usual.

ISABEL. No you don't! A hell of a lot more than usual, and don't deny it because it's getting to be pretty obvious. I mean I know he gets on your nerves. I knew that the first day we met. But it's more than that now. These past couple of meetings I've caught you looking at him, watching him in a . . . I don't know . . . in a sort of hard way. Very critical. Not just once. Many times. Do you know you're doing it? (*Shrug of the shoulders from* THAMI.) Well if you know it or not, you are. And now he's started as well.

THAMI. What do you mean?

ISABEL. He's watching you.

THAMI. So? He can watch me as much as he likes. I've got nothing to hide. Even if I had he'd be the last person to find out. He sees nothing, Isabel.

ISABEL. I think you are very wrong.

THAMI. No, I'm not. That's his trouble. He's got eyes and ears but he sees nothing and hears nothing.

ISABEL. Go on. Please. (*Pause.*) I mean it, Thami. I want to know what's going on.

78

THAMI. He is out of touch with what is really happening to us blacks and the way we feel about things. He thinks the world is still the way it was when he was young. It's not! It's different now, but he's too blind to see it. He doesn't open his eyes and ears and see what is happening around him or listen to what people are saying.

ISABEL. What are they saying?

THAMI. They've got no patience left, Isabel. They want change. They want it now!

ISABEL. But he agrees with that. He never stops saying it himself.

THAMI. No. His ideas about change are the old-fashioned ones. And what have they achieved? Nothing. We are worse off now than we ever were. The people don't want to listen to his kind of talk any more.

ISABEL. I'm still lost, Thami. What kind of talk is that?

THAMI. You've just heard it, Isabel. It calls our struggle vandalism and lawless behaviour. It's the sort of talk that expects us to do nothing and wait quietly for White South Africa to wake up. If we listen to it our grandchildren still won't know what it means to be free.

ISABEL. And those old-fashioned ideas of his . . . are we one of them?

THAMI. What do you mean?

ISABEL. You and me. The competition.

THAMI. Let's change the subject, Isabel. (*Takes up his notebook*.) Charles Dickens . . . Thomas Hardy . . . Jane Austen.

ISABEL. No! You can't do that! I'm involved. I've got a right to know. Are we an old-fashioned idea?

79

THAMI. Not our friendship. That is our decision, our choice.

ISABEL. And the competition.

THAMI (*uncertain of himself*). Maybe . . . I'm not sure. I need time to think about it.

ISABEL (*foreboding*). Oh boy. This doesn't sound so good. You've got to talk to him, Thami.

THAMI. He won't listen.

ISABEL. Make him listen!

THAMI. It doesn't work that way with us, Isabel. You can't just stand up and tell your teacher he's got the wrong ideas.

ISABEL. Well, that's just your bad luck because you are going to have to do it. Even if it means breaking sacred rules and traditions, you have got to stand up and have it out with him. I don't think you realize what all of this means to him. It's a hell of a lot more than just an 'old-fashioned idea' as far as he's concerned. This competition, you and me, but especially you, Thami Mbikwana, has become a sort of crowning achievement to his life as a teacher. It's become a sort of symbol for him, and if it were to all suddenly collapse . . . ! No. I don't want to think about it.

THAMI (*flash of anger and impatience*). Then don't! Please leave it alone now and just let's go on with whatever it is we've got to do.

ISABEL. Right, if that's the way you want it . . . (*Takes up her notebook.*) . . . Charles Dickens, Thomas Hardy, Jane Austen . . . who else?

THAMI. I'm sorry. I know you're only trying to help, but you've got to understand that it's not just a personal issue between him and me. That would be easy. I don't think I

80

would care then. Just wait for the end of the year and then get out of that classroom and that school as fast I can. But there is more to it than that. I've told you before: sitting in a classroom doesn't mean the same thing to me that it does to you. That classroom is a political reality in my life . . . it's a part of the whole political system we're up against and Mr M has chosen to identify himself with it.

ISABEL (*trying a new tack*). All right. I believe you. I accept everything you said . . . about him, your relationship, the situation . . . no arguments. OK? But doesn't all of that only make it still more important that the two of you start talking to each other? I know *he* wants to, but he doesn't know how to start. It's *so* sad . . . because I can see him trying to reach out to you. Show him how it's done. Make the first move. Oh Thami, don't let it go wrong between the two of you. That's just about the worst thing I could imagine. We all need each other.

THAMI. I don't need him.

ISABEL. I think you do, just as much as he . . .

THAMI (*his anger flaring*). Don't tell me what I need, Isabel! And stop telling me what to do! You don't know what my life is about, so keep your advice to yourself.

ISABEL (*deeply hurt*). I'm sorry. I don't mean to interfere. I thought we were a team and that what involved you two concerned me as well. I'll mind my own business in future. (*She collects her things.*) Let's leave it at that then. See you next week . . . I hope! (*Starts to leave, stops, returns and confronts him.*) You used the word friendship a few minutes ago. It's a beautiful word and I'll do anything to make it true for us. But don't let's cheat, Thami. If we can't be open and honest with each other and say what is in our hearts, we've got no right to use it. (*She leaves.*)

Warrior
Shirley Gee

Based on the story of Hannah Snell, known as the Female Soldier, who was born in Worcester in 1723 and, after many adventures, died in Bedlam in 1792. In this scene Hannah is 18, married to a sailor, David Snell, and living in the house of her sister-in-law, Susan. Susan is described as 'worn, impatient, sensible, cross & loving', and is older than Hannah. Hannah is a visionary, passionate and brave, boyish but feminine; her accent should have a roughened edge.

Time: mid-eighteenth century.

Susan's house.

HANNAH (*a scream*). DAVEY! (HANNAH *stands alone, in her nightshift. She holds a letter.*) Oh, no. DAVEY! (SUSAN *enters, startled out of sleep.*) Oh, Susan. (*She holds out the letter. Susan takes it.*)

SUSAN. 'Dear one. I'm not meant to be stuck ashore. I've signed back on the *Cloud*.' The dog. 'Sorry about the two pound. Never fear. I'll come back rich as a king, your loving Davey.' The double dog. Gambling again?

HANNAH. He promised me. He swore.

SUSAN. He'd eat a live cat for a wager. Two pound?

HANNAH. A bit above.

SUSAN. How in God's earth will you find two pound?

HANNAH. I don't know, do I? I'd pledge the spoons, but there's no spoons left to pledge.

SUSAN. You've nothing?

HANNAH. Less than nothing.

SUSAN. Well, I'm sorry Hannah, but I have to say it. You've dug your own pit. Always a shilling behind, that's you. What'll you do? They'll come after you. They will. It'll be prison, Hannah.

HANNAH (*looking round wildly*). There's the clock. That's ours. And . . . and . . . (*She can't see anything else.*) and . . . (*She takes off her locket.*)

SUSAN. Six shillings. Seven at most.

HANNAH. What'll I do? I don't know what to do.

SUSAN. No use looking to me and Caleb, we can't help.

HANNAH. Course not. We're living on you as it is.

SUSAN. Not that we grudge you, mind. After all, he is my brother. Even if he is the back end of a dog. And you're a good soul, Hannah.

HANNAH. Lord, I'm afraid of prison.

SUSAN. Cassie Terson cut her throat because her husband ran off with her savings. Whatever will you do?

HANNAH. When he comes back I'll crack his head for him so hard.

SUSAN. Comes back? He's forgotten you already.

HANNAH. Never.

SUSAN. Did he tell you he was going?

HANNAH. No.

SUSAN. Well then.

HANNAH. I think he tried. He cried in my arms last night.

SUSAN. Well he might.

HANNAH. I can feel his tears on the back of my hand.

SUSAN. Without your man you're nothing. Lost your place. (HANNAH *staggers suddenly, covers her eyes with her hands a moment, takes her hands away, stares.*) What is it? What –

HANNAH. The sea. The sea. It's everywhere.

SUSAN. Oh my Lord.

HANNAH. There's Davey standing in it, at the edge. He's staring at me. Oh, his eyes are sad. Now his shadow's left him . . . and turned white . . . and sank beneath the waves.

SUSAN. I hate it when you're like this.

HANNAH. There's blood in the sea. Drops of blood, like ladybirds, on him. He's sinking now. He's gone.

SUSAN. Oh, Hannah, you do frighten me. (HANNAH *dives suddenly for a clothes chest, starts to haul clothes out.*) What are you doing now?

HANNAH. Going after him. He'll drown. I have to stop him.

SUSAN. You can't. Hannah, you can't. (HANNAH *is pulling on a shirt.*) It's only a dream.

HANNAH. I don't dream. I see.

SUSAN (*of the shirt*). That's Caleb's.

HANNAH. He'll get it back.

SUSAN. It's his best.

HANNAH. It's not. It's the other one. (*Tugging on long johns.*) You know it's a warning. Remember the bolting horse? And the fire? And the night your father died? I saw them all. He mustn't go to sea. (*As* SUSAN *starts to speak.*) I
84

know. They're Caleb's too. I'd have worn Davey's but he's took them all.

SUSAN. Let him go. He's worthless.

HANNAH. He's good at heart.

SUSAN. All because of some stupid, stupid dream –

HANNAH. Do you want the sea to have him? (*She puts on shoes and stockings.*)

SUSAN. You never stop to think. He's had the night's start. What if he's sailed already?

HANNAH. Then I'll go to sea as a sailor. Follow him.

SUSAN. You don't know anything about the sea.

HANNAH. The sea is blue. And deep.

SUSAN. And you've to watch it for it's after you to pull you down.

HANNAH. I've learnt to make a soup and light a fire and pledge a thing I haven't got. (*Cramming hair into a cap.*) I'll soon get used to it.

SUSAN. Sailors are demons.

HANNAH. Davey's a sailor.

SUSAN. They live in sin and blood. And die in it. What if you get swept up in a war?

HANNAH (*dressed now*). How'll I do?

SUSAN. You wouldn't fool a rabbit.

HANNAH. Is it here? (*Her breasts.*)

SUSAN. It's all of you. Anyone could tell with half an eye.

85

HANNAH. I do swell, don't I. (*She reaches to the chest, pulls out a long piece of cloth, takes off her shirt, wraps it round.*) Tie it. Oh, quick, Suke. Please. (SUSAN *ties the cloth tight.*) I can't be a man, but I can be a boy.

SUSAN. Man or boy, you'll have to breathe. How do you think you're going to manage among all those men?

HANNAH. I'll snarl and spit and march about a bit. (*Dressed again, she rolls a seaman's sock of Davey's, uses it for a codpiece.*) How's that?

SUSAN. Better. Much. How'll you do at night?

HANNAH. Snore. Belch. Fart. I shall fart all night if I want.

SUSAN. Hannah, you can't.

HANNAH. I can do anything. Once you're a man you can kick the world like a king. (*She collects a few things – a mug, candles, matches, a knife, bundles them into a man's jacket.*)

SUSAN. You're determined, then?

HANNAH. Like iron. Don't worry, Suke. Soon as he sees me, he'll come back.

SUSAN. You must be careful.

HANNAH. I will.

SUSAN (*crying*). You mustn't cry, no matter what.

HANNAH (*not crying*). I won't.

SUSAN. You must be gruff.

HANNAH (*gruff*). I will.

SUSAN. Better still, be silent. (HANNAH *nods.*) And grim. (HANNAH *nods grimly.*) You are the best . . . the . . .

stupidest sister-in-law a body could ever . . . If anyone finds you out . . . oh, feel my heart. Leave it a week and see.

HANNAH. I can't. How can I? (*She sees Davey's kerchief sticking out of his trousers pocket, pulls it out, is sad. She recovers, and ties it round her neck.*) I'll find him and I'll bring him back and there's my mind and there's the end of it. (*She marches upstage, turns.*) The sea shan't have him. (*She salutes.*) Everything strong and hearty.

SUSAN (*calling after her as she goes*). Hannah! You're off to the slaughter-house.

HANNAH. Not I. I'll sail like the moon in the sky. (SUSAN *exits. As* HANNAH *crosses and recrosses the stage she becomes more confident, more at home in her clothes. She kicks at stones, tries to whistle, fails, succeeds at last and is delighted with herself. She exits.*)

A Proper Little Nooryeff
Leonard Gregory
(*from the novel by Jean Ure*)

Jamie, a sporty, likeable 15-year-old has been discovered to have a talent for ballet and is coerced into helping out for a performance in aid of charity. Anita, also 15, is dedicated, single-minded, almost obsessive about a career in ballet. They are in the rehearsal room at Miss Tucker's Dancing school. Jamie, in normal street gear, is sprawled in a chair, trying hard to avoid eye contact with Anita who faces him dressed in leotard and tights. They are waiting for Miss Tucker.
   Time: The present.

ANITA. What's the matter with you? Why haven't you got changed? (*Pause.*) Jamie, Miss Tucker's going to be here any minute. You know she doesn't like wasting time. We have come here to dance, you know!

JAMIE. Is that all you ever think about? Dancing?

ANITA. No, of course it isn't! But just at this moment . . .

JAMIE. So what else do you think about?

ANITA. Lots of things. Loads of things!

JAMIE. Tell me some.

ANITA. Jamie, this is not the time!

JAMIE. Do you ever think about the bomb and people starving and what it's like not to have money?

ANITA. Yes . . . sometimes. But now is not the . . .

JAMIE. You mean like once a year, maybe? Or once in two years?
88

ANITA. Well, how often do you?

JAMIE. More than you, I bet. Do you know, I've never heard you talk about anything that wasn't ballet?

ANITA. It's not because I'm not interested in other things. It's just that if you want to be a dancer there simply isn't room for anything else. If you really want to get anywhere . . .

JAMIE. Crap!

ANITA. Jamie, it's not crap! It's true! Imagine if you wanted to be a footballer, or a cricketer, or a . . . a pop star, or something. Imagine how hard you'd have to work . . . all those training sessions – all the practice. Well, it's exactly the same with dancing. It's just no *use* thinking you can skip class every time you're feeling a bit off or something a bit more interesting turns up. You have to put ballet first.

JAMIE. Yeah – that's if you're going to be a dancer.

ANITA. I'm sure you could be, if you wanted. If you tried for ballet school . . .

JAMIE. Me? I'm not trying for any ballet school! My old man would have a fit.

ANITA. Is that the only thing that stops you?

JAMIE. No, it is not! If you want to know the truth, I don't reckon I ought to be doing this lot. (*There is a pause.* ANITA *looks at him.*)

ANITA. Why not? (JAMIE *gets up and moves moodily about the room.* ANITA *watches him.*)

JAMIE. I dunno. Just doesn't seem . . . right. I s'pose.

ANITA. What do you mean, it doesn't seem right? What doesn't seem right?

JAMIE. This dancing lark. My Dad . . . (*Anita waits.*) My Dad reckons dancers are a load of old nannies.

ANITA. Oh, well! Your Dad! It's the stupid sort of thing someone's Dad would say, isn't it? I bet *your Dad* doesn't know the first thing about it . . . I bet he couldn't tell an *entrechat* from an *arabesque*. (JAMIE *says nothing.*) I suppose it would be all right if you wanted to be a boxer. That's manly, isn't it? Two men knocking the life out of each other . . . that's really manly, that is. (JAMIE *maintains his silence. Trying another tack.*) Warriors dance. Look at African tribes – look at Zulus. Look at Cossacks! What about the Red Army? It's always the men.

JAMIE. It's different for them.

ANITA. How? Dancing's dancing, isn't it? (*Pause.*) Miss Tucker said we'd have trouble. She said you'd think it was compromising your masculinity.

JAMIE. I don't think it's compromising my masculinity.

ANITA. All right, then! So if you're not scared that it's poufy and that people are going to laugh at you, why don't you want to do it? (*Pause.*) It's because you *are* scared that they're going to laugh at you! You are, and you just won't admit it! You're such a coward!

JAMIE. No, I'm not.

ANITA. Yes, you are! It bothers you, what other people think. *You* don't think it's poufy, but . . .

JAMIE. How do you know? How do you know I don't?

ANITA. Because if you did you wouldn't be any good at it. And you are good at it. Miss Tucker thinks you could really get somewhere if you were prepared to work.

JAMIE. Yeah, well, I'm not. Not at dancing, at any rate . . .

Please, sir! I'm going to ballet school . . . Doug would die laughing.

ANITA. You mean you'd sooner spend your life doing some boring, soulless job in a factory than be a dancer?

JAMIE. Who says I'm going to do some boring soulless job in a factory?

ANITA. All right! So what are you going to do?

JAMIE. I'm going to play cricket . . . and what's more, I'm going to play it on Saturday.

ANITA. Saturday? But that's the day of the show!

JAMIE. I know.

ANITA. So how can you possibly play cricket?

JAMIE. Look, I already told you. I am not stopping playing cricket for you or anyone else.

ANITA. Jamie, I know you think I'm just being stupid and making a fuss, but I'm not. Honestly, I'm not! I'm really *not*. You've only got to sprain something, or pull a muscle, or even just bruise yourself . . .

JAMIE. So what are you suggesting? I should wear a suit of armour?

ANITA. Imagine if you got knocked out!

JAMIE. Then you'd have to dance with Garstin, wouldn't you?

ANITA. I wouldn't dance with Garstin if he were the last man left on earth! I wouldn't be seen dead on the same stage with Garstin!

JAMIE. So that's your problem. I can't guarantee I'm not going to get knocked stone cold. It's a chance you'll have to take.

ANITA. You mean you really are going to play?

JAMIE. You'd better believe it. And as a matter of fact, I'm not even certain I'm going to be able to make the dress rehearsal on time. We've got a net practice that goes on till seven on Friday evening. I might just be able to get there for seven-thirty. On the other hand, I might not. (*There is a long pause.*)

ANITA. You'd better tell Miss Tucker.

JAMIE. Don't worry. I will. (*As* JAMIE *speaks,* MISS TUCKER *and the* PIANIST *enter.* ANITA *looks hard at* JAMIE, *who avoids her stare.*)

Murmuring Judges
David Hare

The title derives from a legal expression meaning 'to speak ill of the judiciary'. Irina Platt, a black lawyer in her mid-twenties, is involved in her first case which brings her into contact with a criminal justice system and some dubious personalities. Sandra Bingham, a WPC also in her mid-twenties, small, tidy, blonde and 'a high-flyer', is also involved on the case but experience has taught her to be cautious and cool. The two women meet outside in south London, near the Crystal Palace.
Time: The present.

Crystal Palace. IRINA is standing at the top of the hill, right by the great radio mast. She is slightly hidden. Below her, London is laid out, glimmering at dusk on a summer evening. The wind is blowing gently, the air is light. Then SANDRA appears in blue jeans and a blouson, walking through the park. IRINA steps out where SANDRA can see her. SANDRA stops.

IRINA. No, it's not chance. (SANDRA *looks at her a moment.*)

SANDRA. What is this? (IRINA *doesn't answer.*) I know who you are. I saw you . . .

IRINA. Yes.

SANDRA. At that trial. I don't have to talk to you.

IRINA. No.

SANDRA. It's against the rules.

IRINA. Well, loosely. Technically, yes. (IRINA *waits to see if* SANDRA *will go on.*)

93

SANDRA. You know I can shop you.

IRINA. Sure. I'm aware of that.

SANDRA. Improper approaches.

IRINA. I've not said a thing.

SANDRA. Not yet.

IRINA. I don't think you'd shop me.

SANDRA. Wouldn't I?

IRINA. No.

SANDRA. Why not? You've chosen a woman. Does that make you feel safer? Why didn't you choose Jimmy? Or Barry? You thought I'd be easier. I sort of resent that. (*For the first time they both smile.*)

IRINA. You're free. You don't have to stay. (SANDRA *looks at her a moment, then makes a little move, just a few paces away, to look out over London.* IRINA *waits.*) So. Is this where you live?

SANDRA. Nearby. Selhurst Park. When I was a kid we walked over this hill every week. To watch Crystal Palace.

IRINA. Is that the sports team?

SANDRA. Yes. They play football.

IRINA. Ah, yes. I've done my best to understand England, but some of the nuances pass me right by. (SANDRA *smiles at this.*)

SANDRA. Crystal Palace don't have many nuances. (*But* IRINA *is not fazed; she just goes on talking gently.*)

IRINA. Is football an interest of yours?

94

SANDRA. It was my Dad. He used to take me. He'd walk me over the hill to eat fish and chips. I'd stand outside the pub while he had a couple of lagers. (*She smiles.*) He was trying to bring me up as a boy.

IRINA. Oh dear . . .

SANDRA. No, it was nice . . . at least when I discovered. I'd kind of taken it for granted I was male. But that made it specially interesting, you know, when I was fourteen or fifteen. And I found out that I was a girl.

IRINA. Was your Dad a copper?

SANDRA. Yes.

IRINA. I guessed.

SANDRA. Is it really that obvious? (*They both laugh.*) He was great. He had this brilliant idea. That policing was really exciting. He said you're out on your own. Your own boss. It's you and the public. There's no one to tell you you're getting it wrong. You learn on the job. You learn by doing it. Each time you go out, you start over. It's you and them. (*She stops and thinks a moment.*) He complained. But he never stopped loving it.

IRINA. And is that how you feel?

SANDRA. Oh, yeah, it's great. It's great while you're doing it. But it's sometimes hard to come home. (*She gives her a slightly nervous glance, her real feelings on show, and* IRINA *picks up on her tone.*)

IRINA. You know why I'm here?

SANDRA. Probably.

IRINA. It's this terible frustration of knowing something . . . something tricky has happened and then not being able to find any proof. (SANDRA *looks at her impassively, not giving anything away.*) You see, I know . . . I know there was some sort of fiddle . . .

SANDRA. Go on.

IRINA. I know what occurred.

SANDRA. You don't *know*.

IRINA. No. I can guess. (SANDRA *still doesn't react.*) But until I can find that one individual . . . I need an individual . . . I need a friend inside the police.

SANDRA. Yes. I can see. (SANDRA *looks at her a moment, then moves away slightly.*)

IRINA My client got beaten up.

SANDRA. Yes. I heard that. (*There's a pause,* IRINA *confident that she has Sandra's interest.*) Why did that happen?

IRINA. To shut him up.

SANDRA. Are you sure? Any witnesses? (IRINA *shakes her head.*) Well, then you haven't a case.

IRINA. No. (SANDRA *shrugs slightly, but* IRINA *knows she is still hooked.*) I'm in trouble at work because of this. They say it's a quite unexceptional case. Which it is. To me that's the point. (*She is suddenly quiet.*) But they have a way of making you feel you're a bore and an idiot for wanting the truth of something. Do you know that feeling?

SANDRA. No. Never had it.

IRINA. You see, when you're training, it's the great cliché. A lawyer should never be emotionally involved. Not a day goes by when they don't mention this. 'Only a bad advocate gets too close to his case.' They love it, they say it over and over. It's like they can't say it enough. They say it a thousand times. They say it so often you turn round and think . . . now what exactly are you trying to hide? (SANDRA *frowns*.)

SANDRA. But it's true.

IRINA. Is it?

SANDRA. Sure.

IRINA. To me it's the alibi. It's the great alibi.

SANDRA. It's being a professional.

IRINA. Is that what it is? (*She smiles*.)

SANDRA. It's like in the police. I know, I've been through this. You let a lot by. You have to.

IRINA. Do you?

SANDRA. Yeah. Yeah. Certainly. Or else you'd go crazy. (SANDRA *looks at her, unapologetic.* IRINA *is quiet again*.)

IRINA. So how do you choose when it's time to say no? (SANDRA *looks at her for a moment now.* IRINA *makes a slight move towards her with a card*.) I've written my number here. In case you want to call me.

SANDRA. Thank you.

IRINA. In case you decided . . . you might change your mind. (SANDRA *takes the card, not moving yet*.) I was going to walk out. Yes. At one point. This was just a week or two ago. I thought, I can't take it here. Then I thought, if I go, just how exactly will that help my client? And the answer is, not at all. (*She smiles*.) I don't know, I was thinking I should move to radical chambers. There's something they call the alternative bar. Perhaps it would suit me better. (*She looks and sees* SANDRA *has a smile on her face*.) Why are you smiling? What are you smiling at? (SANDRA *just shakes her*

97

head, a real warmth suddenly between the two women.) Please tell me.

SANDRA. Because there's nothing called the alternative police.

IRINA. No . . . (*They both smile together, joined by the thought.*) No, I know that . . .

SANDRA. There isn't a kind of nice lot who all read the *Guardian* and eat salad for lunch . . . (IRINA *smiles.*) You can't join another lot. Not in my profession. You see, in my line of work there's only one crowd. (*The two women smile, a little diffidently. Then they head off separately, small against the vastness of the evening.*)

IRINA. Goodbye, Sandra. Good luck.

The Day After the Fair
Frank Harvey
(*from the short story by* Thomas Hardy)

Edith Harnham, an attractive woman in her thirties 'with a certain nervous vitality suggesting concealed tension', is not very happy in her marriage to an older man. She has befriended her very pretty, impetuous 18 year old maid, Anna, almost taking on the role of a mother. Anna is illiterate and Edith is writing letters for her to send to Charles, a young man from a class above her whom she met at the Fair. Edith finds herself growing more and more attracted to him through the letters. They are in the front room of the Harnhams' house in a West Country cathedral city.

Time: late nineteenth century.

EDITH. Let me see what you've done. (ANNA *hands the copy-book to* EDITH *who studies it for a moment.*) Anna, this is *not* good enough. It really isn't. I can't believe you're even trying.

ANNA. I am, ma'am, truly I am. It's just that I can't do it like you, ma'am.

EDITH. But with the copy staring you in the face surely it's not too much to ask you to *spell* the words correctly. Look – you've left the *e* out of Charles all the way down the page.

ANNA. Have I, ma'am?

EDITH. Yes, you have.

ANNA. I didn't mean to, ma'am.

EDITH. It's just carelessness. The fact is you're not putting your mind to it. (*Desperately.*) And you must, Anna, you must! I'd have thought, for the sake of someone you say you love, you'd have been only too anxious to work hard at your writing. If you're not prepared to make even this small sacrifice, then what kind of a wife are you going to be, Anna?

ANNA (*rather sullenly*). Once you're married, what'll it all matter?

EDITH. That may well be something you've yet to discover. But you're *not* married, Anna – not yet. There are nearly four more weeks until the wedding-day, and that means at least seven or eight *more* letters have still to be written. *Who* is going to write *them*?

ANNA. Well – you'll have to, ma'am, I suppose.

EDITH. Oh, if only you'd made more progress, Anna. Even if I'd had to help you with the sentiments, at least you could have written the letters yourself. As it is – (*She drops the copy-book on to the desk.*) – there's only one thing I can do.

ANNA. How do you mean, ma'am?

EDITH. He must be told, of course. He must be told everything.

ANNA (*alarmed*). No, ma'am.

EDITH (*firmly*). He must be told that all this time, I've been answering his letters for you.

ANNA. But why, ma'am? Why do you have to tell him now?

EDITH. Because, once you're married, he's bound to find out – sooner or later. Then think of all the miserable recriminations that would begin . . .

ANNA. But if you tell him now, ma'am, he might change his mind and not marry me at all.

EDITH. That should be for him to decide, Anna. And the poor fellow must be given the opportunity to do so in the full knowledge of all the circumstances.

ANNA (*distressed*). Oh, ma'am! But what would I *do*? What would *happen* to me? I think if he was to change his mind now I'd – I'd make an end to myself.

EDITH. Anna! Don't ever say such a wicked thing!

ANNA. I would, ma'am. For what kind of a life should I look forward to?

EDITH. But can't you see that a marriage built on a deceit – on a mere trick, if you like – because that's how it'll seem to him – could so easily become the most bitter and loveless existence imaginable?

ANNA. But once we're married, I shan't need to worry about the old letters because I know, from going with him, I can make him happy. I know that. And at those times, ma'am, he's never bothering himself about grammar or spellin' or fine words or any things like that.

EDITH (*stung*). There are other times to consider, Anna. And let me tell you this: it was the *letters* and *only* the letters that made him decide to marry you.

ANNA. No! No, it wasn't, ma'am, it wasn't.

EDITH. *My* letters, Anna.

ANNA. But it's me he wants – not old letters. Over and over, he's told me that. It's *me*.

EDITH. Oh yes, in a physical sense, I'm sure he finds you wholly desirable. I don't doubt that for a moment. But to give his sudden passion some lasting value, he was looking for something more. Well, he found it – in my letters.

ANNA. You *say* that.

EDITH. He told me. (ANNA *is deeply upset.*)

EDITH. So now you see, don't you, how terribly wicked it would be not to tell him the truth? (*A sullen silence from* ANNA.) You do see, don't you?

ANNA (*stoutly*). No, I *don't* see. How can letters matter, whatever you put, set beside what the two of us have been to each other?

EDITH. If you'd shown more concern for what was written in the letters instead of leaving it all to me, you'd not ask such a foolish question.

ANNA. I tried – I did try to at the start, only in the end they were always written your way.

EDITH. Yes, but *his* letters? Why, apart from wanting to know when he was coming again, you've never shown the slightest interest in his letters, either.

ANNA. It's just that I've grown to feel they're not much to do with me.

EDITH. No. And in a sense, they're not. But Mr Bradford doesn't feel that. Each letter from him has marked a step forward to which I always had to respond. So it's not you he's come to know, Anna, but me.

ANNA. Only in his head. But me – he knows me. He *really* knows me. He's never even touched you.

EDITH. I don't care, Anna. I cannot go on. I shouldn't go on. And it's not only him I'm thinking of – I'm thinking of the effect it's having on me.

ANNA. On you, ma'am?

EDITH. Yes.

ANNA. But it can't have any effect on *you*, ma'am.

EDITH. How can you say that?

ANNA. Because . . .

EDITH. Well?

ANNA. Because you're married already.

EDITH. Oh, you poor, stupid little fool! Can't you see what it's meant to me to have had to write to this man for weeks on end? And to write in terms which are now virtually those of a wife? Can't you see? To have had to lay bare my deepest, most intimate feelings and then – oh, God! – pretend – pretend to a physical condition which, in fact, isn't mine at all? Can you imagine what that's meant to me and still say it can't have had any effect on me?

ANNA. But, ma'am . . .

EDITH. Every letter from him, I read as if it were meant for me. Every letter I wrote was written from *my* heart and nobody else's. And I won him, Anna. *I* won him.

ANNA (*desperately*). You didn't! You didn't!

EDITH (*almost shouting in Anna's ear*). Do you think a man like him would have let himself be captured by a common, ignorant servant girl? (ANNA *flinches and hides her face.*) Those were *my* thoughts and *my* feelings he responded to, and for the first time in my life I feel I'm no longer alone. I've someone to love and care about – even though to him I'm hardly so much as a name. But it cannot go on – it cannot go on. (EDITH, *overcome, sinks down and sobs. For a moment* ANNA *struggles mentally with the dimly perceived implications of* EDITH's *words, then she moves quickly to her mistress and kneels beside her.*)

ANNA. I haven't rightly understood. But now I see – of course. (*Pause.*) You love him too, don't you?

Beautiful Thing
Jonathan Harvey

Steven lives with his brutal, drunken father, but moves in next-door with Jamie and his mother when things get bad. A relationship develops between the boys. Jamie is almost 16, a plain looking lad, timid and unsporty. Ste at 16 is attractive, altogether rougher and tougher. The flats are part of a south London housing estate. It is mid-afternoon on a hot summer day and Jamie is sitting on the step of his flat, cleaning his glasses when Ste enters. Both are dressed in school uniform.

Time: The present.

JAMIE. Hiya.

STE. Oright?

JAMIE. Bunkin' off?

STE. No, I'm at school, what's it look like?

JAMIE. Not like you.

STE. It's only Sports Day.

JAMIE. Not like you to miss a race.

STE. First time for everything.

JAMIE. You're in the relay team.

STE. Yeah well . . . don't wanna put . . . put strain on me ankle. It's . . . injured in training.

JAMIE. Oh.

STE. S'not the end of the world.

JAMIE. I was gonna stay and watch you, then Miss Penrose said you'd pulled out so I came back here. Told me Mum it wasn't compulsory. Sports Day.

STE. Thassa big word init?

JAMIE. Compulsory? I know.

STE. I been down Tavy Bridge.

JAMIE. Get anything?

STE. Nah, skint.

JAMIE. I aint seen ya. Where you been hiding?

STE. Nowhere.

JAMIE. Knocked for you a few times.

STE. I aint been hiding.

JAMIE. Thought you mighta come round.

STE. I aint been hiding, all right? It's hot, bloody heat wave Jamie, and you expect me to be indoors?

JAMIE. No, it's just, you know, just a bit weird.

STE. I was out. All right? What's weird about that? I wan' hiding. I was just, you know, out.

JAMIE. Been worried about ya.

STE. Don't be.

JAMIE. Well I was.

STE. Well don't be!

JAMIE. Have they . . . ?

STE. No.

JAMIE. What?

STE. Nothing's happened. Yeah? I'm all right. I'm pucker. Everything . . . everything's pucker.

JAMIE. You aint running coz you're black and blue. That's why init? I know. I've seen. That's why you aint in the relay team.

STE. Give it a rest Jamie.

JAMIE. Oh things getting better then are they? Life a bowl o'cherries in the end flat? Daddy laid off the fist work? Or haven't you burnt the tea lately?

STE. I said leave it out.

JAMIE. You're scared.

STE. I aint scared o'nothin'!

JAMIE. Yeah?

STE. Yeah! Last week, right. I went Woolwich. Comin' out of a shop and there's this geezer in the gutter, pissed out of his skull, lying there. And everyone was just walking past him. I had to step over him. (*Pause.*) And it was my old man. (*Pause.*) Got me thinking on the bus. Why be scared of a bloke who's dead to the world?

JAMIE. When he knocks ten different types o'shite outa ya.

STE. He's an embarrassment. Nothing more, nothing less. Why be scared o'that?

JAMIE. Scared o'being called queer?

STE (*pause*). Are you?

JAMIE (*pause*). Dunno. Maybe. Maybe not.

STE. And are you?

JAMIE. Queer?

STE. Gay.

JAMIE. I'm very happy. (*Pause.*) I'm happy when I'm with you. (*Pause.*) There, I've said it now haven't I? Go on, piss yourself.

STE. No.

JAMIE. Why not? Don't you think it's funny?

STE. I don't wanna.

JAMIE. I think it's hilarious.

STE. Yeah?

JAMIE. Too right.

STE. Well why aren't you laughin' then?

JAMIE (*pause*). D'you wanna come round tonight? (*Pause.*) 'No Jamie, I don't!'

STE. I got a tongue in me head!

JAMIE. Well say somin' then.

STE. Can't.

JAMIE. Well say no then.

STE. Let's do somin'.

JAMIE. What?

STE. Let's go the park and have a kick-about.

JAMIE. Football?

STE. Yeah, go and get your new ball.

JAMIE. What?

STE. Come on Jamie, I can't hang around here all day it does me head in. (JAMIE *disappears inside. He returns quickly* *with the football* TONY *bought him earlier. He stands in the doorway holding it.*)

STE. Come on then, on the head son! (STE *angles to do a header,* JAMIE *keeps the ball.*)

JAMIE. I can't.

STE. Jay . . .

JAMIE. I'm crap.

STE. That's coz you never try.

JAMIE. I hate football.

STE. Just kick it. (JAMIE *tuts and kicks the ball to* STE.) No you're doing it wrong. Like this. (*Kick it back to* JAMIE, *demonstrating a proper kick.* JAMIE *kicks it back again.*) Yeah that's more like it. Keep your foot like this, it's all in the angle. (*They kick the ball between them.*)

JAMIE. Are you gonna come round then?

STE. I don't know.

JAMIE. Go on. Come round.

STE. Jamie.

JAMIE (*they carry on kicking as they speak*). Is this how Gary Lineker started d'you think?

STE. What? Like you?

JAMIE. Yeah?

STE. If I remember rightly Jamie, whenever we had football in juniors, you ran up and down the field playing 'Cagney and Lacey'.

JAMIE. Shut up.
108

STE. You used to row with Neil Robinson over who was gonna play the blonde.

JAMIE. You mean Cagney, Chris Cagney. (*Adopts an American accent, in imitation of Chris Cagney.*) My name's Christine Cagney and . . . and I'm an alcoholic.

STE. You never went near the ball.

JAMIE. Gary Lineker was just the same!

STE. Yeah?

JAMIE. Yeah.

STE. Which one was he then?

JAMIE. Lacey, the fat one.

STE (*laughs*). He ain't fat.

JAMIE. I know.

STE. He's pucker.

JAMIE. I know, he's all right inn'e? (*Giggles, keeps the ball and reverts to his Cagney impersonation.*) I dunno Marybeth . . . I . . . I just don't seem to be able to find the right kinda guy. They take one look at me, a cop in a pink fluffy jumper, and just . . . back off.

STE. Oh Christine Cagney, you make me heart bleed!

The Children's Hour
Lillian Hellman

The author considered this 'really not a play about lesbianism, but about a lie.' A schoolgirl spreads a rumour that the two principals of the Wright-Dobie School for Girls have an unnatural relationship. The results are devastating. Pupils are removed from the school by anxious parents and Karen's engagement to Dr Joe Cardin becomes vulnerable. Karen is 28, attractive and with a warmth and pleasant manner that made her popular with the students. Martha, the same age, was always the more nervous and highly strung. They are in the school living room, in a country area, 18 miles from the town of Lancet, USA.

Time: 1930s.

After a moment MARTHA *comes in with small tray and dust-cloth.*

MARTHA (*goes to lamp on* D. L. *table, lights it*). It gets dark so early now. (*Crosses to desk, puts down tray, empties ashtray into it.*) Cooking always makes me feel better. I found some purple scylla for the table. Remember! They were the first things we planted here. And I made a small cake. Know what? I found a bottle of wine. We'll have a good dinner. (*Crosses to below* R. *end of sofa, picks newspaper up from floor. No answer. She crosses back to above desk.*) Where's Joe?

KAREN. Gone.

MARTHA (*puts newspaper on desk*). A patient? Will he be back in time for dinner?

KAREN. No.

MARTHA (*watching her*). We'll wait dinner for him, then. Karen! What's the matter?

KAREN (*in a dull tone*). He won't be back.

MARTHA (*speaking slowly, carefully*). You mean he won't be back any more tonight? (*Slowly crossing L. above desk.*)

KAREN. He won't be back at all.

MARTHA (*quickly, walks to R. of KAREN*). What happened? (*KAREN shakes head.*) What happened, Karen?

KAREN. He thought we had been lovers.

MARTHA (*tensely*). I don't believe you. I don't believe it. What kind of awful talk is that? I don't believe you. *I don't believe it.*

KAREN. All right, all right.

MARTHA. Didn't you tell him? For God's sake, didn't you tell him it wasn't true?

KAREN. Yes.

MARTHA. He didn't believe you?

KAREN. I guess he believed me.

MARTHA (*moves upstage. Angrily*). Then what have you done? It's all wrong. It's crazy. I don't understand what you've done. You 'guess' that he believed you. (*Comes back to R. of KAREN.*) There's no guessing about it. Why didn't you – ?

KAREN. I don't want ever to talk about it, Martha.

MARTHA (*sits in chair L. of desk*). Oh God, I wanted that for you so much!

KAREN. Don't carry on. I don't feel well.

MARTHA. What's happened to us? What's really happened to us?

III

KAREN. I don't know. I think I'll make a cup of tea and go to bed now.

MARTHA. Whatever happened, go back to Joe. It's too much for you this way.

KAREN (*irritably*). Stop talking about it. Let's pack and get out of here. Let's take the train in the morning.

MARTHA. The train to where?

KAREN. I don't know. Some place; any place.

MARTHA. A job? Money!

KAREN. In a big place we could get something to do.

MARTHA. They'd know about us. We've been in the headlines. We're very famous.

KAREN. A small town, then.

MARTHA. They'd know more about us, I guess.

KAREN. We'll find a place to go.

MARTHA. I don't think we will. Not really. I feel as if I couldn't move, and what would be the use? It seems to me I'll be sitting the rest of my life, wondering what happened. It's a bad night, tonight, but we might as well get used to it. They'll all be like this.

KAREN (*gets up, goes to stove. Hands in front of it, warming herself*). But it isn't a new sin they tell us we've done. Other people aren't destroyed by it.

MARTHA. They are the people who believe in it, who want it, who've chosen it for themselves. That must be very different. We aren't like that. We don't love each other. We don't love each other. We've been close to each other, of
112

course. I've loved you like a friend, the way thousands of women feel about other women.

KAREN (*Turns her back to stove*). I'm cold.

MARTHA. You were a dear friend who was loved, that's all. Certainly there's nothing wrong with that. It's perfectly natural that I should be fond of you. Why, we've known each other since we were seventeen and I always thought –

KAREN (*as if she were tired*). Why are you saying all this?

MARTHA. Because I love you.

KAREN. (*sits on* D. L. *chair*). Yes, of course. I love you, too.

MARTHA. But maybe I love you *that* way. The way they said I loved you. I don't know – Listen to me.

KAREN. What?

MARTHA (*kneels down next to* KAREN). *I have loved you the way they said.*

KAREN (*idly*). Martha, we're both so tired. Please don't –

MARTHA. There's always been something wrong. Always – as long as I can remember. But I never knew it until all this happened.

KAREN (*for first time looks up, horrified, turns to* MARTHA). Stop that crazy talk –

MARTHA. You're afraid of hearing it; I'm more afraid than you.

KAREN (*turns away, hands over her ears*). I won't listen to you.

MARTHA. You've got to know it. I can't keep it to myself any longer. I've got to tell you that I'm guilty.

KAREN (*deliberately*). You are guilty of nothing.

113

MARTHA. I've been telling myself that since the night we heard the child say it. I lie in bed night after night praying that it isn't true. But I know about it now. It's there. I don't know how. I don't know why. But I did love you. I do love you. I resented your marriage; maybe because I wanted you; maybe I wanted you all these years; I couldn't call it by a name but maybe it's been there ever since I first knew you –

KAREN (*tensely, grips arms of chair*). It's not the truth. Not a word of it. We never thought of each other that way.

MARTHA (*bitterly*). No, of course *you* didn't. But who says I didn't? I never felt that way about anybody but you. I've never loved a man – (*Stops. Softly.*) I never knew why before. Maybe it's that.

KAREN (*carefully*). You are tired and sick.

MARTHA (*as though talking to herself*). It's funny. It's all mixed up. There's something in you and you don't do anything about it because you don't know it's there. Suddenly a little girl gets bored and tells a lie – and there, that night, you see it for the first time, and you say it yourself, did she see it, did she sense it – ?

KAREN (*turns to* MARTHA. *Desperately*). What are you saying? You know it could have been any lie. She was looking for anything –

MARTHA. Yes, but why this one? She found the lie with the ounce of truth. I guess they always do. I've ruined your life and I've ruined my own. I swear I didn't know it, I swear I didn't mean it – (*Rises, crosses* U. L. *In a wail.*) Oh, I feel so God-damned sick and dirty – I can't stand it any more.

KAREN. All this isn't true. We don't have to remember it was ever said. Tomorrow we'll pick ourslves up and –

MARTHA. I don't want tomorrow. It's a bad word.

KAREN (*who is crying*). Go and lie down, Martha. And in a few minutes, I'll make some tea and bring it to you. You'll feel better.

MARTHA (*looks around room, slowly, carefully. She is now very quiet. Moves, turns, looks at* KAREN). Don't bring me any tea. Thank you. Good night, darling. (MARTHA *exits* L. KAREN *sits alone without moving. There is no sound in the house, until, a few moments after* MARTHA's *exit, a shot is heard. The sound of the shot should not be too loud or too strong, the act has not been sensational. For a few seconds after the noise has died out,* KAREN *does not move. Then, suddenly, she springs from chair, and runs out* L.)

The Wakefield Mysteries
Adrian Henri

*Adapted into modern language from the mystery plays of the Middle
Ages, the text maintains 'the feeling that the actors were workers from
the community playing the Biblical parts'. Satan could be played by an
actor of either sex. The part of Adam has been cut from the opening
speeches, but it is clear that Eve's first words are addressed to him. The
scene is in the Garden of Eden after God has created Adam & Eve.*

EVE. Adam, dear brother . . . husband . . .
This is a place that truly might be called
Paradise.
Yes, go on, love. Explore your
new-found kingdom.
I'll stay here and rest.
Go, don't worry about me,
I'm fine. I wouldn't dare
upset our Maker. (*Exit* ADAM. LUCIFER/SATAN
appears.)

SATAN. What a fearsome fate. Cast in dark dungeons
for evermore. Me and my mates,
my fellow rebels cast in the deepest pit.
The happiness we lost
He's given to this new creation, Man
and Woman, now happy as we should be.
A sight unbearable to me.
Here she is, alone
and open, perhaps, to temptation.
I wonder . . . perhaps I might insinuate
myself . . . in guise of a humble serpent

my lies may sound more convincing . . .
Revenge! (*He moves to the Garden.* EVE *sees him.*)

SATAN. Eve!
Do not fear. I am a lowly creature, a serpent.
One of your humble servants. Here
to do your bidding. All this fruit
looks delicious. Aren't you hungry?
Don't you want to try some?

EVE. They look and smell so good
I can hardly choose between them.

SATAN. Yes, you're almost spoilt for choice.
(*Slyly.*) Mind you, this one here
looks particularly inviting . . .
. . . imagine biting into that.

EVE. Not that one, no!
We've promised not to go
anywhere near it.

SATAN. Why is this so?

EVE. I don't know. Our Master
simply told us not to go
anywhere near.

SATAN. With no reason?
And all this lovely fruit in season?

EVE. No, He just warned of His great anger
if we disobeyed.

SATAN. Eve, listen to me. I may be
only a humble serpent but I am wise
in the ways of this world so new to you.
He has warned you off this tree
because its fruit has a particular property.

Listen carefully. You and your Adam
are children, innocents, knowing
nothing. One bite of this fruit and you will
have Wisdom. There is no poison here,
only Knowledge. Knowledge of everything,
of good and bad, of all things in
this universe. Why do you think
He forbids you this treat?
Worries that you will eat
and know?

EVE. I don't know. Tell me, wise creature.

SATAN. Because He fears your knowledge.
With the help of this tree
you can be as wise, as powerful
as He: you, and Adam.
What a surprise for *him*, when he comes back.
Trust me . . . go on, try . . .

EVE. I don't know . . .

SATAN. Just a little bite . . .

EVE. Well, nothing ventured, nothing gained,
I suppose . . . here goes . . . (*Hesitantly, she takes and bites
the fruit. It tastes good. She eats more.*)

EVE. Mmm. It's good.

SATAN (*who has been exulting in his triumph unseen by* EVE).
What did I tell you?
Now, try it on your husband. (*He sneaks away, enter* ADAM.
He sees her with the fruit.)

EVE. Don't worry, love, this fruit is good. Try some.
. . .we were told
not to eat the fruit because it brings
great blessings. Knowledge, wisdom.
118

We will know as much as Him
Who made us. It's all true,
the serpent told me. A wise creature,
who means us well. We needn't tell,
Adam, love, try some.

The Silver Sword
Stuart Henson
(*from the novel by* Ian Serraillier)

The Balicki family, living in a suburb of Warsaw, Poland, becomes separated in 1940 when Joseph is taken away from his wife and children by the Nazis. He escapes after two years in prison, and walks for over four weeks before arriving in Warsaw to find the school where he had been headmaster and his home in ruins. Jan, a young boy, and a homeless war victim, is small, ragged with fair hair and unnaturally bright eyes.

Time: 1942.

The stage lights dim. One spot remains, isolating Joseph.

JOSEPH. I spent several more days looking for the children. One afternoon while I was poking among the rubble of my old home I found a tiny silver sword. About five inches long, it had a brass hilt engraved with a dragon breathing fire. It was a paper knife that I'd once given to my wife – as a birthday present. (*He looks at the sword sadly then wipes it with care on the sleeve of his coat. He turns, suddenly aware he is being watched.* JAN, *who has entered silently, is squatting on the edge of the spotlight. He has his wooden 'treasure box' in one hand, in the other, a 'travelling box' with a bony grey kitten. Eyeing* JOSEPH *with suspicion,* JAN *turns to his box and lifts out his kitten, as if to say: 'You can't hurt us, we protect each other.' But* JOSEPH *smiles. He steps to him and strokes the kitten.*)

JOSEPH (*gently*). What's his name?

JAN. He hasn't got a name. He's just mine. (JOSEPH *takes the kitten and holds him up admiringly. As he does so* JAN *slips a*

120

hand into JOSEPH's *coat pocket and lifts a wrapped sandwich.* JOSEPH *turns back.* JAN *conceals the theft.*)

JOSEPH. What's *your* name? (JAN *pouts: turns away into the shadow; unwraps and sniffs the sandwich. After a second's thought he skips back close to* JOSEPH.)

JAN. Will you give me that sword?

JOSEPH. But it's mine.

JAN. You found it on my pitch. This is my place.

JOSEPH (*sadly*). No, this is my house – at least this rubble is what's left of it.

JAN. I'll give you food for it. (*Offers* JOSEPH *the sandwich.*)

JOSEPH. No thanks, I have my own. (*Hand to pocket. Pause*). You little thief! (JOSEPH *grabs at the sandwich, but he's holding the kitten.* JAN *steps back and munches at it.*)

JOSEPH (*conciliatory*). Look, maybe you can help me. (JAN *looks suspicious, but pays attention. During the next speech he takes the kitten and returns it to its box.*) I'm searching for my family – three children. Ruth is the eldest – she'd be fifteen now. She's tall and fair. (*He shows the photograph.*) Then Edek, he's thirteen. And Bronia's the youngest – only five. We all lived here. I don't suppose you've seen anything of them.

JAN. Warsaw is full of lost children. They're dirty and starving and they all look alike. (*He turns, and is almost gone when* JOSEPH *calls him back.*)

JOSEPH. Wait! I'll give you this sword on one condition. (JAN *comes back.*) I'm not sure that my children *are* dead. If ever you see Ruth or Edek or Bronia, you must tell them about our meeting. Tell them I'm going to Switzerland to find their mother. To their grandparents' home. Tell them to follow as soon as they can. (*Pause:* JAN *makes no response*). Now, listen. I'm starting off for Switzerland tonight. I don't want to walk all the way, so I'm going to jump a train. Where's the best place? (JAN *holds out his hand for the sword, takes it quickly and hides it in his 'treasure box'*.)

JAN. You will be caught and shot. Or you will freeze to death in the trucks. The nights are bitter. Your hair will be white with frost. Your fingers will turn to icicles. And when the Nazis find you, you will be stiff as the boards at the bottom of the truck. That is what happens to those who jump trains.

JOSEPH. You seem to know a lot about it!

JAN. I've seen it.

JOSEPH. Can't be helped. I must risk it. It's better than going back to the place I've come from.

JAN. I'll take you to the bend where the trains slow down. We must go by the back ways – it's curfew time. If the Nazi patrols see us they'll shoot. (JOSEPH *struggles to keep up with* JAN *as he dashes from point to point in a zig-zag across the stage. Finally they rest, crouching breathless in a dim spot Right*.)

JOSEPH (*after a long pause*). I have much to thank you for and I don't even know your name. (*Another long pause:* JAN *says nothing*.) Have you no parents?

JAN. All I have is my cat, and this box.

JOSEPH. You won't come with me?

JAN (*ignoring the question, opening his box and examining the sword*). This is the best of my treasures. It will bring me luck. And it will bring you luck because you gave it to me. (*Pause*.) I don't usually tell people my name – it's not safe. But because you gave me the sword, I'll tell you. It's Jan.

JOSEPH. There are many Jans in Poland. What's your surname?

JAN. That's all. Just Jan. (*Sound of slow train approaching. JOSEPH stands, looks out into the darkness, back to JAN.*)

JOSEPH. Goodbye Jan. Remember your promise. Whatever happens, I shall not forget you. (*Blackout. The train sound builds to a climax, and fades slowly.*)

Across Oka
Robert Holman

Sixteen-year-old Matty has travelled to Russia with his grandmother to stay with the scientist Pavel, his wife and fourteen-year-old son, Nikolai. The Pavels live on the Oka Reserve and here the boys are involved in an experiment to save the Siberian Crane from extinction. Matty is difficult, at times unpredictable and selfish. Nikolai, although cosseted by his English mother and seemingly naïve, is the more mature when the relationship between the boys crumbles.

   Time: The present.

The dense silver birches of the Oka forest. A large island which the flooding has left. The grass is thick and coarse, and wild with bulrushes. On the ground, between the trees, is a Grey Crane's nest made of twigs and brown grass. A cold, evening sunlight. NIKOLAI enters. He looks towards the nest. MATTY enters. He stops. He puts the incubator down and sits on it.

NIKOLAI. Please do not sit on the incubator. (*MATTY stands up. NIKOLAI runs up the slight incline towards the nest, and kneels down beside it.*)

MATTY. Is that it? (*NIKOLAI picks up a Grey Crane egg from the nest.*)

NIKOLAI. We are here at last, Matty. (*MATTY runs up the incline to the nest. He kneels.*)

MATTY. We've found it.

NIKOLAI. Yes. (*MATTY picks up an egg.*)

MATTY. Where's the mother?

NIKOLAI. Our footsteps will have frightened her away. (NIKOLAI *puts the Grey Crane egg back in the nest.*) Matty, we must not go on like this, you and me. (MATTY *puts his egg back into the nest.*) Are you tired?

MATTY. Yes.

NIKOLAI. I am exhausted by tiredness.

MATTY. Are you feeling all right?

NIKOLAI. No, Matty, I am not. I am finding it all so very hard, my English and everything, and you. (MATTY *looks down.*) This is not right between us. (MATTY *looks up.*)

MATTY. I'm sorry, Nikolai. (NIKOLAI *stands up.*)

NIKOLAI. You must be the cuckoo now. (NIKOLAI *walks to the incubator and carries it back to the nest. He puts it down and kneels.*) Please may I ask you – well, I would like to know if you are the same with your other friends? (MATTY *takes his wristwatch off. He offers it to* NIKOLAI. NIKOLAI *shows the wristwatch on his own arm.*) I do not need it, you know.

MATTY. Well, if I have anything, it's yours. (MATTY *puts his wristwatch back on his arm.*)

NIKOLAI. There is one thing. Please may I ask – well, I would like to ask if you will speak to my mother for me?

MATTY. Yes.

NIKOLAI. Matty, please may I visit you at your home near Middlesborough?

MATTY. Well, of course you may, you idiot.

NIKOLAI. If I ask my mother she will only say 'no'. If you ask her, then I will chip in and be enthusiastic.

MATTY. Yes.

NIKOLAI. I would love to meet your friends and see them for myself. (*A slight pause.*)

MATTY. Well, do you imagine they're all as bad as me?

NIKOLAI. Is Britain a very different country from the Soviet Union? (*A slight pause.*)

MATTY. Yes, I think so.

NIKOLAI. You are very lucky to come here. (*A slight pause.*)

MATTY. I know you don't like me, Nikolai.

NIKOLAI. I think you are a boy who always feels sorry for himself, Matty.

MATTY (*gently*). Do I?

NIKOLAI. Yes, you do. (*A slight pause.*)

MATTY. Do I seem self-pitying?

NIKOLAI. Yes. (*A slight pause.*) Matty, we must be the cuckoo. (NIKOLAI *opens the incubator.*) You must pass me the eggs from the Grey Crane nest. (MATTY *picks up a Grey Crane egg and gives it to* NIKOLAI. NIKOLAI *puts it in the incubator.*) The mother will not be far away, we must be very quick. (MATTY *quickly picks up two more eggs from the Grey Crane's nest.*) Without being slapdash, Matty. (MATTY *slows down. He gives them to* NIKOLAI. NIKOLAI *puts them into the incubator.*) Now you must find the artificial egg from your rucksack. (MATTY *takes off his rucksack. He opens it and finds the pot egg. He gives it to* NIKOLAI. NIKOLAI *puts it in the nest.*) Now, please, you must pass me, very carefully, the fertile eggs of the White Siberian Crane. (MATTY *carefully picks up one of the Siberian Crane eggs. He holds it in his left hand. A slight pause. He offers his right hand to* NIKOLAI. *A slight pause.*)

MATTY. Why not?

NIKOLAI. Matty, I have let you do everything, haven't I?

MATTY. Please, Nikolai. (NIKOLAI *stands up. He moves away. He stops.*)

NIKOLAI. I will come over here, if that is what you want? (*A slight pause.*) Look, I am over here. (*A slight pause.*) They will get cold and the mother will never come back. (*A slight pause.*) Look, Matty. (MATTY *stands up. He offers his hand.*)

MATTY. Why not, Nikolai? (NIKOLAI *hesitates.*) Please.

NIKOLAI. We should go home now, I think. (MATTY *has the egg in his hand.*) Matty, what else can I do?

MATTY. Just shake my hand. (*A slight pause.* NIKOLAI *shakes his head.*)

NIKOLAI. No, you are a very naughty boy. (MATTY *picks up the second Siberian Crane egg from the incubator. He presses his fingers around them.*)

MATTY. I'll break them.

NIKOLAI. No, Matty, you would not do that.

MATTY. I would.

NIKOLAI. Matty, you are a nice boy really. (MATTY *hits the two eggs together. The shells crack. The eggs break. The embryos come out into his hands. Silence.*) Look what you have gone and done. (*Silence.*) You have gone and killed those eggs. How could you go and do that? I hate you. (*Silence.*) I hate you, I hate you, I hate you. I will kick you if you do not give those eggs to me. (NIKOLAI *goes to* MATTY. *He cups his hands.* MATTY *gives him the broken shells and the embryos.*) I will kick you if you do not get out of my sight.

(MATTY *moves away from the nest.*) If you come near me again I will kick you, and kick you, and kick you. (NIKO-LAI *kneels.*) I wish you would get out of my sight I hate you so much. (MATTY *moves away a few more feet. NIKOLAI is looking at the embryos. Silence.*)

MATTY. Is it possible to rescue them?

NIKOLAI. If you talk to me once more I will come over there and kick you. (*Silence.*) No, it is not possible, Matty. (MATTY *has tears in his eyes.*) There's no need to cry as well, you horrible big baby. (NIKOLAI *puts the embryos in the grass.*) If you're going to cry, will you cry away from here. (NIKOLAI *fastens the incubator lid. He stands up. He picks up the incubator.*) I hate you, Matty. (NIKOLAI *goes. MATTY is still, with tears in his eyes. A pause. He begins to sob. He goes to his rucksack and puts it on. He jiggles up and down to get it more comfortable. NIKOLAI enters. He stops. MATTY looks at him.*) Matty, I have decided I must return the Grey Crane eggs to the nest.

MATTY. May I help you?

NIKOLAI. No. Please move away. (MATTY *moves away from the nest. NIKOLAI takes the incubator to the nest. He kneels.*)

MATTY. I'm sorry, Nikolai.

NIKOLAI. I think you are a boy who will always be sorry. I am sorry, too. (NIKOLAI *takes the pot egg from the nest. He stands up.*) I have decided I cannot leave you on your own. (*He goes to* MATTY. *He puts the egg into the rucksack.*) You did not fasten this.

MATTY. Didn't I?

NIKOLAI. No. Our belongings might have fallen out. (NIKOLAI *fastens the rucksack. He goes back to the nest. He* *kneels.* MATTY *goes to the nest.*) I do not want you near me. (MATTY *kneels.*) I think you will always disagree with other people, Matty.

MATTY. If I tell your father, Nikolai. (*A slight pause.*)

NIKOLAI. I do not know what I must tell him.

MATTY. If I tell your father, will you tell my grandmother? She'll kill me.

NIKOLAI. Kill you? Like you killed the Siberian eggs? I do not think your grandmother will kill you, Matty. (*A slight pause.*) This was my father's big trust in me. (NIKOLAI *opens the incubator.*) Do you want her to kill me instead?

MATTY. No. (MATTY *stands up. He walks away from the nest.* NIKOLAI *transfers the Grey Crane eggs. He closes the incubator.*) I wouldn't blame her if she did kill me. (*A slight pause.*)

NIKOLAI. If I tell her it was partly my fault. She will not kill both of us. (NIKOLAI *stands up.*) We could say the Siberian eggs are the ones on the nest, Matty? (*A slight pause.*)

MATTY. What about those? You've just transferred them.

NIKOLAI. I could put them back in the incubator? When we return it would seem the same. (*A pause.*)

MATTY. No. (*A slight pause.*) Well, unless you want to?

NIKOLAI. My father would never forgive me if I lied to him. (NIKOLAI *offers his hand.*) If I shake your hand will you help me tell my father what has happened? (MATTY *slowly walks to* NIKOLAI. NIKOLAI *picks up the incubator.*)

MATTY. I'll tell him, Nikolai. (*The two boys shake hands.*)

The Constant Nymph
Margaret Kennedy and Basil Dean

When their father dies, the gifted Sanger family leave their undisciplined bohemian life in the Austrian Tyrol. A relative, Florence Churchill, aged about 30, becomes their guardian; and arranges school for Tessa, aged 17 and her younger sister. She then marries their adored musician friend, Lewis Dodd, who has always been Tessa's special person. The girls run away from school, the marriage is unhappy and Tessa, a delicate and sensitive girl, cannot cope with Florence's jealousy. The scene is set in the drawing room of the Dodds' house, Strand-on-the-Green, London.

Time: 1925.

TESSA (*hesitates a moment*). Florence! The taxi is here. Charles is waiting. (FLORENCE *stares at her silently.*) Florence! Why are you so cruel to me? You don't mean that I mustn't come to the concert? Not really?

FLORENCE (*still partially stunned*). What?

TESSA (*both hands pressed over her heart*). I won't have palpitations, I won't give any trouble. But Lewis would be so disappointed if – (*The front door is heard to bang.*)

FLORENCE. Lewis is gone.

TESSA. Gone? Oh! (*Bursts into tears.*) And he's never coming back! I never even said good-bye!

FLORENCE. What's that to you? Aren't you ashamed of yourself?

TESSA (*in surprise*). Ashamed?

FLORENCE (*quick and low*). Yes! Ashamed! Do you think I haven't seen – what's been going on all these months? I've seen it and I've tried to ignore it because it's so – so odious. I've tried to excuse you, because you were too young to know what you were doing.

TESSA. What have I been doing?

FLORENCE. I'll speak this once and then we'll never mention this again. Teresa, you must know, that among decent people, that a woman who openly pursues a man, especially a man who doesn't particularly care for her, is despised by everybody. She loses all her dignity and self-respect.

TESSA. What has all this got to do with me? I haven't been pursuing a man who doesn't particularly care for me. I agree with you. It's a mug's game.

FLORENCE. You know perfectly well that you have. It's been perfectly obvious to everyone.

TESSA. I love him very much. I always have. And, perhaps, anyone could see it. But what you say is not true.

FLORENCE. It is true. Your uncle has just spoken of it to me. And – and Lewis himself –

TESSA. Oh, no, Florence. You haven't understood –

FLORENCE. It's odious that I should have to take you to task for your manner to my husband –

TESSA. I'll have to take you to task for your manner to me. I don't think you really mean it, but I won't have those things said to me. It's not my fault that I love Lewis. I did long before you came to the Tyrol. It isn't a happy thing at all. It's brought nothing but sadness into my life. But it's so much all of me that I couldn't want it to be different any

131

more than I could want to be changed into another person. And I've come to understand lately that, now he's your husband, I'd better not see him any more. That's why I've agreed to go away.

FLORENCE. Agreed! You're going because I mean to put an end to this – this disgraceful intrigue.

TESSA (*alarmed*). I don't understand! Intrigue! (*Backing away.*) You're making a mistake. Something terrible has happened! You don't mean all this. Because I love him –

FLORENCE (*taking a step towards her*). Don't you dare speak of love. You don't know what it means.

TESSA (*with a sigh*). I know all about it.

FLORENCE (*her voice rising*). What do you mean by that? (*Seizes* TESSA's *wrists and pushes her back.*) What do you mean? What do you mean?

TESSA. Don't! Don't! What's the matter with you, Florence?

FLORENCE. What do you mean?

TESSA. Don't look at me like that! I've done no harm. What did you think I'd done?

FLORENCE (*almost screaming*). I knew it. I've always known it. You've betrayed me, the pair of you – under my very roof – all these nights – when I thought he was working. In my own house!

TESSA. Well, then, let me get out of your house.

FLORENCE (*beside herself*). How often has he – ? D'you know the name for girls like you?

TESSA (*terrified*). Florence! Stop! I'm not! I'm not!
132

FLORENCE. Yes, you are! You're a harlot! A harlot! Just a common little tart, and nothing else! (CHARLES *is heard calling for* FLORENCE *outside. She throws* TESSA *backwards on the divan and goes out, locking the door.* TESSA *bangs on the door. She runs from the door to the windows in frantic distress.*)

TESSA. Let me out! Oh, let me out! I must get away from this.

My Sister in this House
Wendy Kesselman

Based on a true incident in which two sisters, both maids, murdered their mistress and her daughter in Le Mans, France in 1933. Here Christine, 20, has succeeded in arranging for Lea (pronounced Lēa) not yet 15, to join her in service with Madame Danzard. Two scenes are linked and the shared attic bedroom can be simply staged, with the passing of time marked by music or lighting.
Time: 1930s.

CHRISTINE *and* LEA *pick up shabby suitcases. They smile at each other. They go upstairs to the maid's room. The room is shabby, small. There is a single bed, a night table, a sink and a mirror. There is a small skylight.* LEA *opens the door and rushes into the room.* CHRISTINE *follows her.*

LEA (*excited*). I can't believe it. I just can't believe it. (*She puts her suitcase down on the floor.*) How did you do it? How did you get Maman to agree? Tell me.

CHRISTINE. Shhh. They'll hear you downstairs.

LEA. Tell me. You're always keeping something from me. (CHRISTINE *turns away.*) Tell me.

CHRISTINE (*turning back, smiling*). I told her there'd be more money for her this way.

LEA. You're so clever, so smart.

CHRISTINE. I said that till you learned, you had to have someone to protect you.

LEA. And that was you. That was you. Am I right, Christine? (*She reaches to hug* CHRISTINE.)

134

CHRISTINE (*shivering*). The room's cold. (*She lifts her suitcase onto the bed.*)

LEA. Remember what you used to call me? My feet still get cold at night. They get like ice. (CHRISTINE *opens her suitcase, starts putting her things away. She has few belongings.*)

CHRISTINE (*smiling*). Come on. Put your suitcase up here with mine. I'll unpack it for you. (*She picks up* LEA's *suitcase and puts it on the bed. She begins to unpack it for* LEA.)

LEA. Now they'll be warm. (CHRISTINE *takes a small crocheted blanket out of* LEA's *suitcase.*)

CHRISTINE. What – you still have this old thing?

LEA. I had to take it. She was with me when I packed.

CHRISTINE (*turning away*). Well, I don't care. It has nothing to do with me.

LEA. Don't you like it?

CHRISTINE. It's old and falling apart. I never liked Maman's sewing. It's vulgar. (*Silently, she continues unpacking their things.*)

LEA (*watching her*). What's the matter? Aren't you glad that we're together?

CHRISTINE. Why didn't you take the other room? They offered it to you.

LEA. But I wanted to be with you.

CHRISTINE. The other room was nice. Nicer than this one.

LEA. Christine? (CHRISTINE *is silent.*) I don't understand. You worked the whole thing out and now you don't even want me with you.

CHRISTINE. Of course I want you with me.

LEA. What's wrong then?

CHRISTINE. Nothing's wrong. (*There is a pause.*)

LEA. I'll throw the blanket away if you want. I don't care about it. I just want you to be happy.

CHRISTINE (*finally turning around*). But I am happy, little cold feet. (*She takes the blanket from* LEA.) We'll put the blanket right here. (*She lays the blanket at the foot of the bed.*) The main thing is that now we are together. (*Slowly the light on* CHRISTINE *and* LEA *dims.*)

Scene 2. Early morning. CHRISTINE's *and* LEA's *room is almost dark. They are asleep. The alarm clock rings.* CHRISTINE *turns it off. She reaches out to touch* LEA, *curled up beside her. Gently she touches her shoulder, strokes her hair.*

LEA (*turning toward* CHRISTINE). Is it time?

CHRISTINE. Sleep, turtle. Go back in your shell.

LEA. But –

CHRISTINE. Sleep. There's time. I'll wake you. (LEA *turns over again. She is holding the small blanket their Mother has made.* CHRISTINE *covers* LEA's *shoulder with the blanket. Shivering, she gets out of bed, stands on the cold floor. She puts on her shoes.*) Lea . . . it's almost six.

LEA. Mmmm. Another minute, Christine. Just one more.

CHRISTINE. Just one – all right. (*At the sink, she washes her face and hands. She shivers from the cold water, fixes her hair in the mirror. She removes her long white nightgown and puts on her maid's uniform. She goes over to the bed. Tickling* LEA's *feet.*) Come on now. Come on. (*She pulls the blanket off* LEA.)

136

LEA (*sitting up*). It's freezing here. Is it always like this?

CHRISTINE (*laying out* LEA's *uniform on the bed.*) Always.

LEA. Everywhere you've been?

CHRISTINE. Everywhere.

LEA (*putting on her shoes*). I polished the banister yesterday. Did you notice how it shines?

CHRISTINE. I noticed. (*To herself.*) I thought it would be easier with two of us.

LEA. You're disappointed, aren't you? You're unhappy with me here. Tell me.

CHRISTINE. Don't be silly.

LEA. I can't seem to do anything right. I can't seem to please you.

CHRISTINE. You please me, turtle. You please me more than anything.

LEA. You're so quick. You get things done in a minute.

CHRISTINE. You're fine the way you are.

LEA (*struggling with her nightgown*). Maybe this was a mistake. I slow you down.

CHRISTINE. Stop it, Lea.

LEA (*still struggling*). Sister Veronica always said I was too slow. She said I'd never be as quick as you.

CHRISTINE. What did she know?

LEA. You used to think she knew everything.

CHRISTINE (*helping* LEA *take off her nightgown*). That was a long time ago. I've gotten over all that now.

LEA. You were famous at the convent. Your sewing! They still have that dress you made for the Virgin Mary. She's still wearing it.

CHRISTINE. And yet I remember, when I was at Saint Mary's, I could never go down the stairs like the others. One, two, one, two. I could never take a step with my left foot. It was always my right, my right, my right. I used to envy them running down the stairs when it took me forever.

LEA. Tell me a story, Christine. Just one – before we go down.

CHRISTINE. Which one?

LEA. When I was little.

CHRISTINE. You're still little.

LEA. No, I mean really little – you know – the story with the horse.

CHRISTINE. Again? Don't you ever get tired of it.

LEA. No – tell me.

CHRISTINE (*making the bed*). When you were just a tiny thing, Maman sent me out one day to get bread. You came with me, the way you always did. And as we were walking, you let go of my hand and ran into the street to pick something up.

LEA. Tell it slower. You're telling it too fast.

CHRISTINE. It was a *long* narrow street – you remember – on a hill. At the top of the street a horse and carriage loaded with bottles was coming down and galloping right toward you. I ran into the street and pulled you across and pushed you down into the gutter with me. (*Falling down on the bed with* LEA.) What a noise when the horse galloped by!

138

Everyone was screaming. Maman said the horse had gone mad. And when we stood up, we were both bleeding. But it was the same wound. It started on my arm and went down across your wrist. Look – (*She lines up her arm with* LEA's.) We have it still.

LEA. And Maman – what did she say?

CHRISTINE. Oh Maman. Maman was terrified. You know how her face gets. She screamed at us.

LEA. And then – then what happened?

CHRISTINE. Then there was the gypsy – Mad Flower they used to call her.

LEA. And what did she say?

CHRISTINE. She said – oh you – you know it so well.

LEA. But tell me again, Christine. Tell me again.

CHRISTINE. They're bound for life, Mad Flower said. Bound in blood. (*A bell rings.*)

Wait Until Dark
Frederick Knott

Gloria, a bright, sometimes difficult, bespectacled twelve-year-old, has taken a music-playing doll from Sam and Susy's flat, a doll now known to be a prime clue in a murder case. Susy, an attractive young woman, is blind and, alone in the flat during her husband's absence, becomes caught up in a complex, frightening series of events. Gloria returns from a shopping errand to Susy's Notting Hill Gate basement flat.

Time: Late 1960s.

The stage is empty for several seconds, then we hear someone try the handle of hall door. There is a long pause. Then a key is fitted into the lock and GLORIA creeps in. She is carrying the same large grocery bag that she had before. Seeing no one in the room, she tiptoes down the stairs. She glances through the open bedroom door, then opens the grocery bag and takes out the doll. As though she has already thought this out, she puts the doll carefully on the floor half under the R edge of the sofa, as though it had fallen there by accident. Then she creeps back up the stairs. When she is half-way up SUSY enters from the bedroom. GLORIA freezes still but she is too late and SUSY hears her.

SUSY. Who is that? Mike?

GLORIA (*turning on the stairs*). Oh, hello, Susy!

SUSY (*startled*). Oh! Don't *do* that to me! (*She moves up C.*) How did you get in here?

GLORIA. I borrowed the key you lent Mother. Because when I got upstairs I found I'd left half a pound of butter in the bottom of the bag . . . (SUSY *puts out her hand.*)

SUSY. Thank you, honey.

GLORIA (*coming downstairs to* R *of* SUSY). It's already in the fridge. I closed the door. You can pay me tomorrow, if you like. It came to fifteen-and-fourpence, but you owe me three-and-six from last time, so if I give you one-and-twopence . . . (SUSY *puts her hands up to her ears*.)

SUSY. Don't! No more numbers, please; I'm not a computer. Just call it quits – O,K.?

GLORIA. O.K. Thanks. Bye-bye, then. (*She pauses above the sofa on her way to the stairs*.) It's none of my business, but that man who was in here with Sam's friend . . .

SUSY. That was a Mr Roat. Yes? What about him?

GLORIA. Is he a detective?

SUSY (*very interested*). Why? What makes you think he is?

GLORIA. Because of last night's murder, that's all. (*There is a pause.* SUSY *goes to the kitchen stool*.)

SUSY. Look, poppet, come and stand on this. Can you see through the window? (GLORIA *climbs up on the stool and as she is not high enough she stands on top of the washer and the edge of the sink*.)

GLORIA. Just – I think.

SUSY. There's a police car outside (*She waits*.) You see it?

GLORIA. No.

SUSY. Look carefully. Are you sure?

GLORIA. No police car.

SUSY. It must have gone. There was one there a few minutes ago. Can you see a policeman? Anywhere?

GLORIA. No.

SUSY. Or *anyone* who might be watching this house?

GLORIA. Don't think so. There aren't many people around. It's still raining. (*After a pause.*) Can I get down now?

SUSY. Yes, of course. (GLORIA *starts to climb down.*) Oh, wait a minute. When we first moved in here, Sam used to make his phone calls from a phone box somewhere out there. I think it was near some traffic lights. Can you see a phone box from this window? (GLORIA *climbs up and looks through the window again.*)

GLORIA. Yes, there's one at the end of the road.

SUSY. Is there – a car parked anywhere near the phone box?

GLORIA. One of those Dormobile things – it's right beside it.

SUSY. Anyone in it?

GLORIA. I can't see. It has curtains all around. (*She glances at Susy.*) Is something the matter, Susy? You look awfully worried.

SUSY. It's nothing, love – I'll be all right when Sam gets home.

GLORIA. Would you like me to stay with you until he – (*She looks through the window again and says casually.*) – there's a man getting out now.

SUSY. Out of that car?

GLORIA. Yes – he's talking to someone inside. I can't see who it is. Now he's coming this way . . .

SUSY (*quickly*). Is it Mr Roat? That man who you thought was a detective?

GLORIA. No. It isn't. Sam hasn't done anything, has he? (*She jumps off the stool.*)

142

SUSY. No, of course not. Look, you remember that doll your mother asked you about?

GLORIA. What about it?

SUSY. It belonged to the woman who was killed last night. And if the police found it here they might think that Sam had something to do with it. (GLORIA *sees* CROKER *approaching to peer in at the window. She runs R.*) That's why it's so important . . .

GLORIA. Look out! (*She ducks down R of the sofa.*)

SUSY. What is it? (CROKER *peers in, but cannot see* GLORIA *or the doll.*)

GLORIA (*in a whisper*). There's a man looking through the window. (SUSY *goes over to sink and pretends to be cleaning up.*)

SUSY (*without moving her lips*). Can he see you?

GLORIA. No. But he's still looking. It's the man from the Dormobile. (*Very cautiously,* GLORIA *feels for the doll and then drags it carefully behind the sofa. As she does this, it plays two or three notes of its tune.* SUSY *hears this and turns sharply.* CROKER *leaves the window.* GLORIA *peeps cautiously over sofa.*)

SUSY (*horrified*). Don't let him see the doll! (SUSY *backs to the left wall and closes the blackout across both windows.*)

GLORIA. He's gone now. (*There is a pause, then the street doorbell rings.*)

SUSY. That's the street door! And it's locked. Run up and see if you can lock the back door. (GLORIA *grabs doll and runs half-way up the stairs, then halts.*)

GLORIA. We can't. I think Daddy took the key with him. And it hasn't got any bolts. (*The street doorbell rings again.*)

SUSY. We've got to hide that doll quickly! Anywhere!

GLORIA (*running up*). I'll take it upstairs.

SUSY. No! (*Taking out the garbage pail.*) In here! (GLORIA *runs downstairs and stuffs the doll back in the grocery bag, twists the top shut and hides it in the garbage pail.*) Where on earth did you find it?

GLORIA (*innocently*). It was just lying under the table by the settee. It must have fallen off . . .

SUSY (*sharply*). We've been searching this room for over an hour. You've got to tell me.

GLORIA (*after a pause*). I took it. (*The street doorbell rings.*)

SUSY. Why?

GLORIA. When I first saw it in here, I thought it was a present for me, but Sam said it was for another little girl. So – I stole it. It's in the sanibin. You can't possibly see it.

SUSY (*very quickly, but with tremendous emphasis*). How would you like to do something that's difficult – and terribly dangerous?

GLORIA. Yes! What?

SUSY. Can you see that call-box – from upstairs?

GLORIA. From mother's bedroom – I think.

SUSY (*pointing to the phone*). Write down our phone number quickly. (GLORIA *goes to the phone and copies the number down, using the paper and pencil on the table.*) Now listen very carefully – this is difficult. Go upstairs and watch that call-box and don't take your eyes off it. Not for a second. (*Slowly.*) Now if *anyone* from the Dormobile goes in and makes a phone call – phone me the moment he comes out again. Do you understand?

GLORIA (*as if it was nothing*). Yes – I understand. (*She crosses R.*)

SUSY. *Only* the Dormobile people – and only when he has come *out* of the call-box.

GLORIA. No problem. (*She starts up the stairs.*)

SUSY. No, wait, I've got a better idea. When you phone me I won't answer. Just let it ring *twice*. And then hang up.

GLORIA (*coming down to* SUSY). I know. Like a signal. There's a friend of Daddy's who does that. Only *she* does it seven times. (*She starts upstairs again, then turns and says in a whisper.*) Susy, if you need me for anything just bang on the water-pipe. You can hear it all over the house. (CROKER *is heard opening the back door.*)

SUSY. Where is it?

GLORIA (*returning to* SUSY). By the stove. I'll show you. (GLORIA *starts leading Susy to the pipe up* L. *The hall doorbell rings.* SUSY *holds* GLORIA *by the shoulders to keep her from moving.*)

SUSY (*calling*). Who is it?

GLORIA. Detective-Sergeant Croker.

SUSY (*calling*). Just a second, please. I'm on the phone. I won't be a moment. (GLORIA *pulls* SUSY's *head down, whispers something in her ear.* SUSY *nods and* GLORIA *quietly tiptoes into the cupboard under the stairs and closes the door. To cover* GLORIA's *movements* SUSY *pretends to be speaking on the phone.*) That's a wonderful idea – and a box of Kleenex and a large bottle of aspirin . . . That's all, darling – I'll have to go now. There's someone at the door. 'Bye. (SUSY *goes upstairs and opens the door.*) I'm sorry I kept you waiting.

145

Tartuffe
Moliere
(*translated by* R Wilbur and A Drury)

Orgon, infatuated with Tartuffe, a middle-aged hypocrite, 'round and red', wishes his daughter Mariane to marry him. Mariane, though loving Valère, finds it hard to oppose her dominant parent. Dorine, her maid, a sparky, sharp-tongued girl, takes control of the situation. This scene takes place in Orgon's Paris house.

Time: 1660s.

DORINE (*returning*). Well, have you lost your tongue, girl? Must I play
Your part, and say the lines you ought to say?
Faced with a fate so hideous and absurd,
Can you not utter one dissenting word?

MARIANE. What good would it do? A father's power is great.

DORINE. Resist him now, or it will be too late.

MARIANE. But . . .

DORINE. Tell him one cannot love at a father's whim;
That you shall marry for yourself, not him;
That since it's you who are to be the bride,
It's you, not he, who must be satisfied;
And that if his Tartuffe is so sublime,
He's free to marry him at any time.

MARIANE. I've bowed so long to Father's strict control,
I couldn't oppose him now, to save my soul.

DORINE. Come, come, Mariane. Do listen to reason, won't you?
Valère has asked your hand. Do you love him, or don't you?

MARIANE. Oh, how unjust of you! What can you mean
By asking such a question, dear Dorine?
You know the depth of my affection for him;
I've told you a hundred times how I adore him.

DORINE. I don't believe in everything I hear;
Who knows if your professions were sincere?

MARIANE. They were, Dorine, and you do me wrong to doubt it;
Heaven knows that I've been all too frank about it.

DORINE. You love him, then?

MARIANE.   Oh, more than I can express.

DORINE. And he, I take it, cares for you no less?

MARIANE. I think so.

DORINE.   And you both, with equal fire,
Burn to be married?

MARIANE.   That is our one desire.

DORINE. What of Tartuffe, then? What of your father's plan?

MARIANE. I'll kill myself, if I'm forced to wed that man.

DORINE. I hadn't thought of that recourse. How splendid!
Just die, and all your troubles will be ended!
A fine solution. Oh, it maddens me
To hear you talk in that self-pitying key.

MARIANE. Dorine, how harsh you are! It's most unfair.
You have no sympathy for my despair.

147

DORINE. I've none at all for people who talk drivel
And, faced with difficulties, whine and snivel.

MARIANE. No doubt I'm timid, but it would be
wrong . . .

DORINE. True love requires a heart that's firm and strong.

MARIANE. I'm strong in my affection for Valère,
But coping with my father is his affair.

DORINE. But if your father's brain has grown so cracked
Over his dear Tartuffe that he can retract
His blessing, though your wedding-day was named,
It's surely not Valère who's to be blamed.

MARIANE. If I defied my father, as you suggest,
Would it not seem unmaidenly, at best?
Shall I defend my love at the expense
Of brazenness and disobedience?
Shall I parade my heart's desires, and flaunt . . .

DORINE. No, I ask nothing of you. Clearly you want
To be Madame Tartuffe, and I feel bound
Not to oppose a wish so very sound.
What right have I to criticize the match?
Indeed, my dear, the man's a brilliant catch.
Monsieur Tartuffe! Now, there's a man of weight!
Yes, yes, Monsieur Tartuffe, I'm bound to state,
Is quite a person; that's not to be denied:
'Twill be no little thing to be his bride.
The world already rings with his renown;
He's a great noble – in his native town;
His ears are red, he has a pink complexion,
And all in all, he'll suit you to perfection.

MARIANE. Dear God!

DORINE. Oh, how triumphant you will feel
At having caught a husband so ideal!

MARIANE. Oh, do stop teasing, and use your cleverness
To get me out of this appalling mess.
Advise me, and I'll do whatever you say.

DORINE. Ah no, a dutiful daughter must obey
Her father, even if he weds her to an ape.
You've a bright future; why struggle to escape?
Tartuffe will take you back where his family lives,
To a small town aswarm with relatives –
Uncle and cousins whom you'll be charmed to meet.
You'll be received at once by the elite,
Calling upon the bailiff's wife, no less –
Even, perhaps, upon the mayoress,
Who'll sit you down in the *best* kitchen chair
Then, once a year, you'll dance at the village fair
To the drone of bagpipes – two of them, in fact –
And see a puppet-show, or an animal act.
Your husband . . .

MARIANE.   Oh, you turn my blood to ice!
Stop torturing me, and give me your advice.

DORINE (*threatening to go*). Your servant, Madam.

MARIANE.   Dorine, I beg of you . . .

DORINE. No, you deserve it; this marriage must go through.

MARIANE. Dorine!

DORINE.   No.

MARIANE.   Not Tartuffe! You know I think him . . .

DORINE. Tartuffe's your cup of tea, and you shall drink him.

MARIANE. I've always told you everything, and relied . . .

DORINE. No. You deserve to be tartuffified.

MARIANE. Well, since you mock me and refuse to care,
I'll henceforth seek my solace in despair:
Despair shall be my counsellor and friend,
And help me bring my sorrows to an end.
(*She starts to leave.*)

DORINE. There now, come back; my anger has subsided.
You do deserve some pity, I've decided.

MARIANE. Dorine, if Father makes me undergo
This dreadful martyrdom, I'll die, I know.

DORINE. Don't fret; it won't be difficult to discover
Some plan of action . . . But here's Valère, your lover.

Two Weeks with the Queen
Mary Morris
(*from the novel by* Morris Gleitzman)

Colin, an Australian boy, about 14, has been sent to relatives in England, because his younger brother, Luke, is dying of cancer. His cousin, Alistair, the same age, is an inexperienced 'Mummy's boy' both awed and scared by Colin's assertiveness. The scene takes place in Alistair's parents' sitting room. A London suburb.
Time: The present.

ALISTAIR. Colin?

COLIN. What?

ALISTAIR. Have you really ridden a trail bike, or were you pulling my leg?

COLIN. Straight up. Yamaha 250. Twin exhaust, cross-country gear ratios.

ALISTAIR. Brill.

COLIN. Yeh, it was alright till the brakes failed and I went over the cliff.

ALISTAIR. You went over a cliff?

COLIN. Yeh. But it's OK, the ocean was underneath, broke my fall.

ALISTAIR. The Pacific Ocean?

COLIN. Yeh. The surf wasn't too high, only fifteen metres or so.

ALISTAIR. Brill.

COLIN. 'Course the sharks were a problem.

ALISTAIR. Sharks!

COLIN. White pointers. There were a couple of them. Reminded me of the time I had to fight crocs off in the Territory.

ALISTAIR. Crocodiles?

COLIN. Twenty-footers. I gave them a wrestle for their money, but.

ALISTAIR. Do you know Crocodile Dundee?

COLIN. He's a mate of mine, gave me a few tips. See, a croc's got no brains. You can outsmart 'em. Not like sharks. Only way with sharks is to out-swim them.

ALISTAIR. You can out-swim sharks?

COLIN. All Australians can. Wouldn't be any of us left if we couldn't. Alistair, don't you ever get bored?

ALISTAIR. No. Well, a bit. Sometimes.

COLIN. How would you like to help me save Luke's life?

ALISTAIR. I'm not allowed to give blood!

COLIN. You don't have to give blood. Listen, do you reckon the Queen's doctor would be the best doctor in the world?

ALISTAIR. Yes, pretty good, specially cos he'd have to do it without looking.

COLIN. Eh?

ALISTAIR. Well, he would, wouldn't he? I mean if the Queen was sick he couldn't just say, 'take your frock off your Majesty and let me look at your . . . er . . . your . . . you know', could he? I mean, not the Queen. Nobody could,

could they? He'd have to guess what's wrong. He'd have to be good.

COLIN. Er . . . yeh. Anyway, I wrote to her and asked her to let me get in touch with him, and she didn't write back.

ALISTAIR. When did you write to her?

COLIN. Nearly a week ago.

ALISTAIR. Well, there you are then. It'll be months before she gets round to it.

COLIN. She a bit slack?

ALISTAIR. No, not her. But hundreds of people write to her. She gets sackfuls of letters every day. Special vans full of letters for her.

COLIN. I've seen them. They've got Royal Mail written on them.

ALISTAIR. Er, yeh. Takes a bit of time to answer all them letters.

COLIN. Well, I haven't got time, I'm going to have to get into the palace and talk to her myself. And you're gonna help me.

ALISTAIR. You want me to help you break into Buckingham Palace?!

COLIN. Someone has to give me a leg up.

ALISTAIR. Mum doesn't let me go into town by myself.

COLIN. You won't be by yourself, you'll be with me.

ALISTAIR. But you can't just climb into the palace, there'll be alarms and dogs and stuff.

COLIN. No there won't, well only corgis and they'll be asleep on the Queen's bed.

ALISTAIR. How do you know?

COLIN. It was in our papers at home. A few years ago, a bloke got into Buckingham Palace at night and next morning, when the Queen woke up he was sitting on the end of her bed, looking at her. He didn't have a single dog bite on him.

ALISTAIR. I remember that.

COLIN. If he can do it, we can.

ALISTAIR. They put him in a loony bin.

COLIN. Alright then! I'll do it myself.

ALISTAIR. I'll come.

COLIN. OK, we'll set the alarm tonight for three-thirty in the morning.

ALISTAIR. I'll stay.

COLIN. Don't be a wimp.

ALISTAIR. What if you get shot?

COLIN. OK stay then!

ALISTAIR. I'll come.

COLIN. Good one. Three-thirty then. Let's go and buy a rope. (*They start to go.*)

ALISTAIR. But I'm not allowed out in the traffic.

COLIN. Alistair, anybody'd think a bus was gonna jump the kerb and weave through all the other shoppers, carefully avoiding rubbish bins and brick walls and flatten you!

ALISTAIR. Well, one could do, couldn't it?

COLIN. Alright, I'll go and buy the rope myself.

ALISTAIR. I'll come.

A Game of Soldiers
Jan Needle

Sarah, Michael and Thomas are three children living on Falkland Island during the Falklands War. They are playing 'Soldiers' when they discover a wounded Argentinian soldier. They decide they should kill him, though Sarah remains doubtful and insists on going to her house for a blanket and food to give him some comfort before he dies. Michael, 13, and Thomas, 8, are left alone, in their den, by the sea.
Time: 1980s.

The sea den. MICHAEL *and* THOMAS *enter, talking.*

MICHAEL (*as they come in*). It's great this, isn't it? It's not a game any more. It's real. Absolutely ace.

THOMAS. Do you think she'll do it, though? Do you think she'll go through with it?

MICHAEL. She promised, didn't she? She swore like the rest of us? Death to the enemy! Fantastic.

THOMAS. She only swore when you gave in, though. It seems daft to me, to get him food and drink and blankets. Then to kill him. It's potty.

MICHAEL. Female logic, Thomas. There's no rhyme or reason to it. But never mind, it does no harm to humour them. That's what my father always says.

THOMAS. I could see her point in a way. I mean, him with the gun and that. And us with nothing. It might lull him into a . . . you know. . . . Mightn't it?

MICHAEL. A sense of false security. Yeah, I s'pose it might. He might even go off to kip if he's got some food in

155

him, and a nice warm blanket on. That'd make life easier. For us.

THOMAS (*rather daring; he's subtly taunting* MICHAEL). And she didn't give you a lot of choice, in the end, did she? Take it or leave it, she said, suit yourself. It was. . . .

MICHAEL. Don't kid yourself, son. I'd have talked her round. But she had a point, I've said so, haven't I? A sense of false security. (*Pause.*)

THOMAS. Michael?

MICHAEL. Yeah?

THOMAS. How you. . . . How we. . . . What exactly are we going to do? To . . . you know . . . kill him?

MICHAEL. You're not ducking out are you, Thomas? You're not trying to go back on a swear? Cause if you are. . . .

THOMAS. No, no course I'm not. It's just I. . . . Well, I mean, what exactly are we going to do? How do you kill a man?

MICHAEL. Well, there's lots of ways, aren't there? I mean, it would be easier if he didn't have a gun, we're going to have to be dead careful. Maybe we can let you sneak up on him and snatch the thing away.

THOMAS (*horrified*). What! Me! Sneak up on him!

MICHAEL (*laughs*). I'm pulling your leg, you twit. I wouldn't trust you to take a dummy off a baby. Relax.

THOMAS. Crikey, Michael. Don't say stuff like that! But what if he sees us coming, though? What if he shoots us?

MICHAEL. He won't. That's why I agreed to let Nelly Knickerleg get the food and stuff. I might get my Mum's sleeping pills or something. Put some in his coffee to make
156

sure. Or even some rat poison from the barn. That'd be another way.

THOMAS. But what if they caught you at it?

MICHAEL. They might. That's the problem. But I don't think it's necessary, at all. I think we can do it easier, much easier. (*He takes out his pen-knife and fingers it.*) I tell you what though. I don't half wish this was a real commando knife. That would be the easiest.

THOMAS (*pause, horrified*). Could you knife him, honestly? Groo, I'd throw up. I'd puke.

MICHAEL. I'd stick it in his neck and pull. It'd be sharp as sharp. I'd slice it through his jugular and watch the blood squirt. I could do it.

THOMAS. Hell, Michael. That's horrible.

MICHAEL (*laughs*). It isn't a real knife though, is it? No, it'll be a battering job, I reckon. We'll have to batter him.

THOMAS. How do you reckon to do it? What will you use, a hammer or something? Will you nick one off your Dad?

MICHAEL. 'We', Thomas, not me. No, we won't use a hammer I don't think. Remember where he is. All we've got to do is give him food and keep him occupied. He's in the corner, right? His back's against the wall. While he's noshing, we climb up the outside, or I do, say. Then you or Sarah hands me up a rock. A big one. As big as you can lift. And there you are. We drop it on his bonce. Crunch. A deado. A corpse. Simple. What d'you think?

THOMAS (*hardly audible*). It sounds all right. We'd better stand well clear though. There could be lots of blood. (*Pause.*) It'd be easier, in a way, to let the grown-ups do it, wouldn't it?

MICHAEL. Chicken.

THOMAS. No I'm not. No. But it'll be hell's messy, Michael. We'd better stand well clear.

MICHAEL (*smiles nastily*). You'd better run along now, then, and get the matches, like Aunty Sarah said. And make sure you do, and some paper if you can, to start the fire. That's all we're asking, Thomas. Just matches and paper, to get a fire going. To lull the enemy. He's going to be comfortable when he dies, this one. *Dead* comfortable.

THOMAS. Yeah. All right then, Michael. I'm off. I've got them in my Lego drawer. My Mum doesn't know. I won't be long.

MICHAEL. You'd better not be. And remember – you were sworn to secrecy as well. Not a word to anyone. Got it?

THOMAS. Yeah, of course I have. Not a word. What are . . . what are you going to do? While we're gone?

MICHAEL. I'll go and stand guard. Just in case. Just in case the enemy's getting frisky. In case he tries to escape. Go on. Off you go. And keep your mouth shut. (THOMAS *goes. After a pause,* MICHAEL *goes also.*)

The Goalkeeper's Revenge
Derek Nicholls and Ray Speakman
(*from the writings of* Bill Naughton)

The play is based on the writings of Bill Naughton, which tell of his lively Lancashire childhood, a time of poverty and unemployment but rich in friendships and shared experiences. Charlie and Bill, close school friends, aged about 13, have suffered under a brutal teacher known as 'Fat Ada'. One day they cut the fruits from her beloved orange plant, a plant that clever Charlie reckoned had 'witnessed cruelty without restraint'. One of her cruel canings was to cause permanent damage. The boys are in a Bolton street, in front of the gable end.

   Time: The 1920s.

In front of the gable end.
Light comes up on BILL. Enter CHARLIE CRIDDLE, one side of his head bandaged.

CHARLIE. Forget thy friends, Bill?

BILL. Charlie!

CHARLIE. How's Fat Ada, Billy?

BILL. Not much changed. Th'art out of hospital, then?

CHARLIE. At last. I'm forbidden school, though.

BILL. Th'art lucky, then.

CHARLIE. What else is a chap to do?

BILL. Plenty. (*Pause.*)

CHARLIE. Has my mam told thee – they've nicked it out? (*Pause.*) An' I'm to have an artificial eye. The best money can buy, says my mam.

BILL. How 'the best'?

CHARLIE. It all festered up, an' the eye doctor said it'd be best to have it out in case it got hold of t'other. I wanted a patch, but my man said I couldn't go round looking like a pirate. 'Artificial eye, the best that money can buy!' I said, 'You're a poet, mam!' He is a fool, an' doesn't know it, who makes himself a craphouse poet. I don't want it favverin' a real eye. Give folk a shock when it ain't. I were reckoning it up, Bill. I know four lads wi' only one eye, an' three grown-ups, one a woman. How many does tha know, Bill?

BILL. I know two lads.

CHARLIE. To talk to?

BILL. One to talk to – one not. Three – did I say two? No, three.

CHARLIE. I've been wondering which eye you wink with when you've a glass un. If you wink with your proper eye, it means you go blind for a time, an' you can't see who you're winking at.

BILL. I know a blind chap, Chey, who can hammer in the dark.

CHARLIE. I were cogitating last night, Bill, about dark an' that. Say you get a field at night covered in darknes – is that just black daylight? I were cogitatin' on an invention called *black* electricity, or *black* gas. Instead of folks havin' to buy blinds, and curtains, and stuff, they just press a button, and there's a bulb or a mantle what comes on full blast with *black* light. Fills every corner of the room with darkness. They could have two switches – white for lighting up, and black for darking up.

BILL. It'd want thinking, Chey.

CHARLIE. Well, think it out. Han they said prayers for me at school?

BILL. They should've. Anyway, we'll be going up to Mr Denning's class for our last few weeks, soon.

CHARLIE. I've told you before, an' I'll tell you again – it were my fault an' not hers. She had nowt to do with it, except she were holding the cane. Fair's fair. Come to think of it, Bill, chap as made the cane were one of the first causes, barring him as planted it. That's the rotter we want to get at. How's the orange tree?

BILL. It'll never lift its head again. Char, I can't agree it's none of her fault. She's to blame, not bloke as made the stick! She's got away with it. Why hast let her? (*Pause.*)

CHARLIE. I wonder will any oranges grow where I planted 'em? They'd be ours, and Fat Ada's by right.

BILL. There's no right, and fair's not fair, Chey. (*no reply*) How is it?

CHARLIE. What?

BILL. Your eye.

CHARLIE. Which eye?

BILL. The one you've had out.

CHARLIE. A daft question, that, Billy. How do I know? I'll bet t'cat's had it by this.

BILL. Where it was.

CHARLIE. Socket. Feels like a factory lodge.

BILL. What, wet?

CHARLIE. Is it heck as wet! It's that flapping big. Her's a damn good teacher, tha knows, Bill.

BILL. Tha calls Fat Ada a good teacher, Chey? After . . .

CHARLIE. My dad were in her class. Course, she were only young then, but she clouted his lug more than once. He used to say to me when he was on leave: 'Tha'll never learn owt, lad, till old Fat Ada gets hold of thee.' He got killed in the war, tha knows. He went through it in the trenches without getting so much as a scratch, an' got himself killed in the last fortnight.

BILL. God rest his soul.

CHARLIE. Thanks. He allus swore by Fat Ada.

BILL. She were responsible, Chey.

CHARLIE. Take these who go to Proddy schools – they never get a real good tanning like we do. And look at 'em – just look at 'em. They'd think the eight beatitudes were a bloody football team. As for things like affinity, consanguinity, and spiritual relationship, they wouldn't know either one of them from a black pudding. Don't say owt against Fat Ada to me.

BILL. But what is consanguinity, Charlie?

CHARLIE. Tha doesn't know what consanguinity is?

BILL. I did know. But I've forgotten.

CHARLIE. Come to that, so have I. Let's away to the woods, Billy. Allez. Touchsweet. (*Fade.*)

P'tang, Yang, Kipperbang
Jack Rosenthal

Alan is 14, a mixture of ordinary schoolboy and sensitive adolescent. Ann at the same age is already more composed, self-contained. In their school play performance Alan fails to kiss Ann at the final dramatic moment. Now, walking home, he is suddenly gravely pre-occupied, beyond tears; Ann is concerned and puzzled. They are in a surburban street of the neighbourhood where they live.
   Time: Summer, 1948.

ANN. *Why*, though, Quack-Quack! Why didn't you do the kiss. You haven't said why. Did you just forget? (ALAN *barely shrugs in reply. She tries again – hopefully.*) I mean there must be a reason. Everything has a reason . . . You can walk me home if you like.

ALAN (*shrugs in reply to* ANN's *invitation*). Alright. (ALAN *and* ANN *walk on, as before.*)

ANN. What do you *think* was the reason?

ALAN. I don't know.

ANN (*trying to jolly him out of his mood*). You don't know much, then, do you!

ALAN (*simply*). No. I don't. I know nothing. (*Pause.*) I used to think I knew everything about everything. The world and that. But I don't. (*Pause.*) Maybe I got it wrong.

ANN. Got *what* wrong?

ALAN. Everything. Tommy. The world. Maybe it's *all* lies.

ANN. What is?

ALAN. Everything I thought. About everything. (*She looks at him. He shivers, involuntarily.*)

ANN. You're shivering.

ALAN. Yes.

ANN. Maybe you're sickening for something.

ALAN. Maybe. (*They walk on in silence. After a moment or two –*) A few weeks ago I trod on a big, fat spider and hundreds of little ones came running out of it. I thought it was perhaps a miracle.

ANN (*hotly*). I don't know about a miracle, it was sodding *cruel*!

ALAN. Accidental.

ANN (*simmering down*). Oh. (*Pause.*) It must just've been pregnant. You just gave it a sort of caesarean.

ALAN. Oh, I see.

ANN. I don't think it'll have been a miracle. It's just Nature, really.

ALAN. Yes.

ANN. Except Nature *is* a miracle, isn't it?

ALAN (*stopping, looks at her, smiles – albeit a little sadly*). Yes. I forgot that. Yes it is. Supposedly. (*They're now at the gate of* ANN's *house. They stand for a moment in silence.*)

ANN. Why didn't you want to kiss me? Am I that grotesque to the nth degree?

ALAN (*looking at her. He speaks quietly, solemnly, completely unselfconsciously, and very, very simply*). You're beautiful, Ann. Sometimes I look at you and you're so beautiful I want to cry. And sometimes you look so beautiful I want to laugh and jump up and down, and run through the streets with no clothes on shouting 'P'tang, yang, kipperbang' in people's letterboxes. (*Pause.*) But mostly you're so beautiful – even if it doesn't make *me* cry it makes my chest cry. Your lips are the most beautiful. Second is your nape.

ANN (*slight pause*). My what?

ALAN. The back of your neck. It's termed the nape.

ANN. Oh, my *nape*.

ALAN. And your skin. When I walk past your desk, I breathe in on purpose to smell your skin. It's the most beautiful smell there is.

ANN. It's only Yardley's.

ALAN. It makes me feel dizzy. Giddy. You smell brand-new. You look brand-new. All of you. The little soft hairs on your arms.

ANN. That's *down*. It's not hairs. It's called down. Girls can have down.

ALAN. But mostly it's your lips. I love your lips. That's why I've *always* wanted to kiss you. Ever since 3B. Just kiss. Not the other things. I don't want to do the other things to you. (*Pause.*) Well, I *do*. *All* the other things. Sometimes I want to do them so much I feel I'm – do you have violin lessons?

ANN (*thrown*). What?

ALAN. On the violin.

ANN. No. Just the recorder. Intermediate, Grade Two.

ALAN. Well, on a violin there's the E string. That's the highest pitched and it's strung very tight and taut, and makes a kind of high, sweet scream. Well, sometimes I want you so much, that's what *I'm* like. (*A pause.*)

ANN (*uncertainly*). Um . . . thank you.

ALAN. I always wanted to tell you you were lovely. Personally, I always think it's dead weedy when Victor Mature – or whatsisname – Stewart Grainger – or someone says a girl's lovely. But you are. (*Pause.*) And I know girls think it's weedy when boys call them sweet. But you are. (*Pause.*) I don't expect I'll ever kiss you now in my whole life. Or take you to the pictures. Or marry you and do the *other* things to you. But I'll never forget you. And how you made me feel. Even when I'm 51 or something. (*A long pause. Whatever else is happening in the street – cars passing, people coming home from work, little kids playing – is unnoticed by them.*)

ANN (*quietly, gently*). Why didn't you kiss me, then?

ALAN. It's like cricketers. Well, I mean, it *isn't* like cricketers. Cyril Washbrook or Denis Compton or any of them . . . They face the bowler – and there are thousands of people watching . . . their families and friends and all the Australian fielders and the umpires and John Arlott and thousands of total strangers. And they don't care. Just keep their eye on the ball and lay their stroke. I don't know how they do it. I couldn't.

ANN (*pause*). Would you like to kiss me *now?* (*He shakes his head sadly.*) No one's watching. (*He shakes his head again.*) Why not? (*Her eyes looking into his,* ANN *starts drying her lips with the back of her hand. Gently,* ALAN *takes her hand away from her lips and holds it by his side. He smiles tenderly at her. A long moment. Then sadly shakes his head.*)

ALAN. I'm sorry, Ann. It's too late.

ANN (*tears starting into her eyes*). It isn't even five o'clock!

ALAN. I didn't mean that. Things are different now.

ANN. Why? What things??

ALAN. You were right, you see, Ann. *Real* men *don't* mess about dreaming. I *could* kiss you . . . but it won't be like I dreamed it'd be. I know it won't. Nothing is. Kids kid themselves. (*A pause.*)

ANN (*hotly*). I think you won't kiss me because I said you *could*!

ALAN. What?

ANN. Because now I *want* you to.

ALAN (*thrown; troubled*). Is that what happens?

ANN. I think you're just being sodding cruel again! Only this time on *purpose*!

ALAN. Don't cry, Ann. *I* used to cry. Even in my sleep . . . dreaming. I won't any more, though. I've jacked in crying now. (ANN *looks into his eyes, bites back tears. Smiles sadly.*)

ANN. Would you like to say P'tang, yang, kipperbang? (*He smiles; shakes his head.*) My favourite words are yellow ochre, burnt sienna and crimson lake.

ALAN. Very nice. (*Pause*). See you tomorrow. (*He turns to go.*)

ANN. Alan? (*He turns back. She kisses him, very briefly, on the cheek.*)

ANN. For good luck, that's all. (*He smiles and starts back down the street. She watches him go for a moment, then turns and goes into her house.*)

Blood Brothers
Willy Russell

Edward and Mickey, though twins, were separated at birth because their mother could not afford to keep both in her poor circumstances. They have never met and are growing up in vastly different backgrounds. The boys are played at all ages through the play by the same two actors and here, meeting for the first time outside Mickey's house, they are 7 years old.

Time: The present.

Bored and petulant, MICKEY aged 'seven' sits and shoots an imaginary Sammy (his older brother). EDWARD, also aged 'seven' appears. He is bright and forthcoming

EDWARD. Hello.

MICKEY (*suspiciously*). Hello.

EDWARD. I've seen you before.

MICKEY. Where?

EDWARD. You were playing with some other boys near my house.

MICKEY. Do you live up in the park?

EDWARD. Yes. Are you going to come and play up there again?

MICKEY. No. I would do but I'm not allowed.

EDWARD. Why?

MICKEY. 'Cos me mam says.

EDWARD. Well, my mummy doesn't allow me to play down here actually.

MICKEY. 'Gis a sweet.

EDWARD. All right. (*He offers a bag from his pocket.*)

MICKEY (*shocked*). What?

EDWARD. Here.

MICKEY (*trying to work out the catch. Suspiciously taking one*). Can I have another one. For our Sammy?

EDWARD. Yes, of course. Take as many as you want.

MICKEY (*taking a handful*). Are you soft?

EDWARD. I don't think so.

MICKEY. Round here if y' ask for a sweet, y' have to ask about, about twenty million times. An' y' know what?

EDWARD (*sitting beside Mickey*). What?

MICKEY. They still don't bleedin' give y' one. Sometimes our Sammy does but y' have to be dead careful if our Sammy gives y' a sweet.

EDWARD. Why?

MICKEY. Cos, if our Sammy gives y' a sweet he's usually weed on it first.

EDWARD (*exploding in giggles*). Oh, that sounds like super fun.

MICKEY. It is. If y' our Sammy.

EDWARD. Do you want to come and play?

MICKEY. I might do. But I'm not playin' now cos I'm pissed off.

EDWARD (*awed*). Pissed off. You say smashing things don't you? Do you know any more words like that?

169

MICKEY. Yeh. Yeh, I know loads of words like that. Y' know, like the 'F' word.

EDWARD (*clueless*). Pardon?

MICKEY. The 'F' word. (EDWARD *is still puzzled. MICKEY looks round to check that he cannot be overheard, then whispers the word to* EDWARD. *The two of them immediately wriggle and giggle with glee.*)

EDWARD. What does it mean?

MICKEY. I don't know. It sounds good though, doesn't it?

EDWARD. Fantastic. When I get home I'll look it up in the dictionary.

MICKEY. In the what?

EDWARD. The dictionary. Don't you know what a dictionary is?

MICKEY. 'Course I do. . . . It's a, it's a thingy innit?

EDWARD. A book which explains the meaning of words. . . .

MICKEY. The meaning of words, yeh. Our Sammy'll be here soon. I hope he's in a good mood. He's dead mean sometimes.

EDWARD. Why?

MICKEY. It's cos he's got a plate in his head.

EDWARD. A plate. In his head?

MICKEY. Yeh. When he was little, me Mam was at work an' our Donna Marie was supposed to be lookin' after him but he fell out the window an' broke his head. So they took him to the hospital an' put a plate in his head.

EDWARD. A plate. A dinner plate?

MICKEY. I don't think so, cos our Sammy's head's not really that big. I think it must have been one of them little plates that you have bread off.

EDWARD. A side plate?

MICKEY. No, it's on the top.

EDWARD. And . . . and can you see the shape of it, in his head.

MICKEY. I suppose, I suppose if y' looked under his hair.

EDWARD (*after a reflective pause*). You know the most smashing things. Will you be my best friend?

MICKEY. Yeh. If y' want.

EDWARD. What's your name?

MICKEY. Michael Johnstone. But everyone calls me Mickey. What's yours?

EDWARD. Edward Lyons.

MICKEY. D' they call y' Eddie?

EDWARD. No.

MICKEY. Well, I will.

EDWARD. Will you?

MICKEY. Yeh. How old are y' Eddie?

EDWARD. Seven.

MICKEY. I'm older than you. I'm nearly eight.

EDWARD. Well, I'm nearly eight, really.

MICKEY. What's your birthday?

EDWARD. July the eighteenth.

MICKEY. So is mine.

EDWARD. Is it really?

MICKEY. Ey, we were born on the same day . . . that means we can be blood brothers. Do you wanna be my blood brother, Eddie?

EDWARD. Yes, please.

MICKEY (*producing a penknife*). It hurts y' know. (*He puts a nick in his hand.*) Now, give us yours. (MICKEY *nicks* EDWARD's *hand, then they clamp hands together.*) See this means that we're blood brothers, an' that we always have to stand by each other. Now you say after me: 'I will always defend my brother'.

EDWARD. I will always defend my brother . . .

MICKEY. And stand by him.

EDWARD. And stand by him.

MICKEY. An' share all my sweets with him.

EDWARD. And share . . .

(SAMMY *leaps in front of them, gun in hand, pointed at them.*)

Kindertransport
Diane Samuels

Eva, a nine-year-old German–Jewish girl is being fostered by Lil Miller in her Manchester home. Desperate for her parents to leave Hamburg and join her in England, Eva slips out of the house one day to look for work for them.

The strong personalities of the distressed, highly intelligent child, and the warm, forthright, outspoken woman are a match for each other.

Scene: Lil's house.

EVA *sneaks in, trying not be seen by* LIL.

LIL (*leaping up. Angry*). You're in then. At last. Good. We have to have a talk, young lady.

(EVA *goes very quiet. Her head droops.*)

LIL. You talk first.

EVA. About what?

LIL. Lying.

EVA. I not know . . .

LIL. Yes you do. Where have you been?

EVA. Alles hängt nur von mir ab. Ich muß einfach. (It's all up to me. I have to.)

LIL. Not the German, Eva.

EVA. Ich muß sie befreien. Außer mir . . . ist keiner . . . da. Niemand da. (I have to get them out. There's no one else.)

LIL. Don't hide behind the German. It won't protect you and you know it.

173

EVA. Sie dürfen mich aber nicht daran hindern. (You mustn't try to stop me. You just mustn't.)

LIL. In English! English!

EVA. Nicht Englisch! Deutsch! Ich bin Deutsche! (Not English! German! I'm German!)

LIL. I've had enough of this, you little snake! Bloody stop it!

EVA (*sobbing*). No good. No good.

LIL. Cut out the snivels! Now! I want facts from you! True ones! Where've you been!

EVA. English lesson.

LIL. How long for?

EVA. Two hours.

LIL. It's half past six now.

EVA. Walk home slow.

LIL. You're not learning English.

EVA. You not like . . .

LIL. If there's one thing I cannot stand, it's a little liar! Where've you been!

EVA. Please . . .

LIL. Now! Before I chuck you out and never let you back in!

EVA. I can't.

LIL. You bloody well better had!

EVA. Promise not to stop me.

LIL. No promises. Truth.

EVA. Please . . .

174

LIL. Now!

EVA. Out walking.

LIL. Where?

EVA. Streets. Knocking on doors.

LIL. What doors?

EVA. Big houses. Rich people.

LIL. Eva!

EVA. I say about (*Pronouncing very carefully.*) Butler and Housekeeper and Chauffeur and Gardener.

LIL. And what do they say?

EVA. 'We have already got.' Or some want to give tea and be sorry. Gentleman gave money at me.

LIL. The shame of it. What on earth d'you think we put an ad in for! To pass the time and have a laugh?

EVA. Sorry.

LIL. Don't you trust me? What good is it if you don't bloody trust me?

EVA. Sorry.

LIL. I took you in didn't I! Said I'd look after you! Why'd you throw it back in my face! Walking the streets like some begging little orphan!

EVA. Do not throw me out. Please.

LIL. Of course I'm not going to throw you out!

EVA. Please. Nowhere else to go.

LIL (*gentler*). Of course I'm not going to throw you out.

EVA. Even if I'm naughty.

LIL. Not even if you're naughty. (LIL *hugs* EVA.)

EVA. Want to be with them.

LIL. You can't be. Not now.

EVA. When?

LIL. Sooner or later.

EVA. I have to get permits.

LIL. Just be glad you're safe.

EVA. What good me to be safe?

LIL. Better than no one being safe, isn't it?

EVA. I must to help . . .

LIL. You are doing.

EVA. But jobs . . .

LIL. . . . are being found for them. (EVA *drops her head*). Be a bit patient won't you? (EVA *shrugs*.) Cheer up and give them out there good reason to be happy. Else what've they got to smile for? (EVA *shrugs*.)

LIL. Well. What've they got?

EVA (*quietly. German*). Nichts.

LIL. What's that?

EVA (*louder. German*). Nichts. Nothing.

LIL. That's right, little getaway. Nothing.

The Monster Garden
Diane Samuels (*from the novel by* Vivien Alcock)

Frances Stein (Frankie), aged 11, daughter of the genetic scientist, Dr Stein, cultivates some jelly from her father's laboratory, and breeds a lovable, but fast-growing baby monster, Monnie. Here she faces the problems that arise from this, with Hazel, her friend of the same age. The girls are in the Steins' garden; it is early evening. Monnie is in a large hut.
   Time: The present.

The Steins' garden. There is now a fully built hutch in the garden. It is early evening. As the scene progresses the light gets dimmer. An open notebook and pencil lie on the ground. FRANKIE and Monnie are by the hutch. FRANKIE sings into the hutch, putting Monnie to sleep. Monnie's music harmonises with FRANKIE's lullaby.

FRANKIE. . . . When the bough breaks the cradle will fall, Down will come baby, cradle and all. (*The music turns into sleeping sounds. FRANKIE hums the lullaby. Sleeping noises are heard spasmodically throughout the scene. FRANKIE sits down, picks up the notebook and concentrates. HAZEL enters.*)

HAZEL. We'll have to get another ball. Can't find it anywhere.

FRANKIE. Shhhh. (*HAZEL reduces her voice to a loud whisper:*)

HAZEL. You got her to sleep!

FRANKIE. You can always tell she's tired when her fingers droop.

HAZEL. Well done.

FRANKIE. I still hate leaving her in that hutch, though.

HAZEL. She's getting used to it.

FRANKIE. I'm not sure . . .

HAZEL. Think how she was today. Playing ball . . . well, until she lost it . . . picking dandelions . . .

FRANKIE. . . . eating dandelions . . . You shouldn't have taught her 'Waltzing Matilda'. Someone will hear.

HAZEL. They'll think it's you. You've got the same sort of voice as her.

FRANKIE. Have I?

HAZEL. All high and out of tune.

FRANKIE. Ha, ha, ha. (*Pause.*)

HAZEL. She's too big for your room now anyway. There's nowhere else for her to go.

FRANKIE. She'll soon be too big for the hutch as well. Yesterday she grew from . . . (*She refers to the notebook.*) 75 centimetres to 81 centimetres.

HAZEL. If she keeps on at that rate she'll be over 2 metres by the time we go back to school.

FRANKIE. And 4 metres by Christmas!

HAZEL. We'll have to do something.

FRANKIE. Ben will know. He'll sort it out. Next week I can show him the record book and he'll be able to work out her rate of growth and all that.

HAZEL. You've not got everything about her in there, have you?

FRANKIE. Only the important things. I've got to keep the notes short – that's what David's always saying. Problem is, I keep wanting to add stuff.

HAZEL. Like what?

FRANKIE. Like what happened today. I mean, should I say that Julia cried when Alf gave Monnie all the food to eat?

HAZEL. Does that count as hard, scientific fact?

FRANKIE. No. Just Julia losing her temper.

HAZEL. So it can't go in. (FRANKIE *looks at what she has just written. Pause.* FRANKIE *thinks.*)

FRANKIE. But, I've started writing it now.

HAZEL. Cross it out then.

FRANKIE. That'll mess it up.

HAZEL. What have you put? (FRANKIE *reads from her record book.*)

FRANKIE. 'Day Eight. Height 81 centimetres. All jelly coating now gone. M shows signs of intelligence, e.g. guessing the flavour, imitation of birds, affection for Frances Stein, counting up to five . . .'

HAZEL. What about me and Alf! You should put in that she likes us too.

FRANKIE. It was only an example.

HAZEL. You can't just say she likes you.

FRANKIE. That's what I mean about scientific notes. You can't put in everything. You've got to choose.

HAZEL. All right. Go on.

FRANKIE. 'Appearance: Handsome.'

HAZEL. I'd say that she was 'unusual', not 'handsome'.

FRANKIE. I think she's handsome.

HAZEL. But that's your opinion.

FRANKIE. And these are my notes.

HAZEL. I can see that.

FRANKIE. Shall I go on?

HAZEL. Sorry.

FRANKIE. 'Growth remains rapid in spite of reduced diet. Julia Hobson accuses Frances Stein of over-feeding. Frances Stein denies this. Hazel Brent confesses she gave M some sweets . . .'

HAZEL. Smarties to be precise. (FRANKIE *pencils in the word 'Smarties'*.)

FRANKIE. Brackets . . . 'Smarties'.

HAZEL. And put that she could tell all the colours just by tasting.

FRANKIE. That's already in under 'guessing the flavour'.

HAZEL. OK.

FRANKIE. '. . . Animal expert Alfred Haynes gives M a good dinner and says he's not going to starve any animal in his care. He says it's cruel and he's not having it. Frances Stein and Hazel Brent agree with him. Julia Hobson . . .' That's when she started crying.

HAZEL. Don't say she lost her temper. Put something else about her. Something she'll like when she reads it. Then she might be a bit nicer tomorrow and we won't have to waste time cheering her up.

FRANKIE. I know . . . (FRANKIE *writes as she speaks*.) 'Julia Hobson kindly donated this book for our record for which we are duly grateful.'

HAZEL. Brilliant. That should keep her happy. (*The sleeping music suddenly becomes anxious cries. FRANKIE rushes to the hutch and puts her hand out as if holding Monnie's hand.*)

FRANKIE. I'm here, Monnie. I'm here. (*Music relaxes. FRANKIE and HAZEL both hum the last two lines of the lullaby. The sleeping music resumes. FRANKIE removes her hand from the hutch and pulls away.*)

FRANKIE. Goodnight little Monnie.

HAZEL. Goodnight. (*HAZEL and FRANKIE creep off.*)

St Joan
Bernard Shaw

Many legends surround the birth, parentage and life story of Joan of Arc. Born around 1411 or 1412, she grew up at Domrémy, in the Lorraine region of France. A devout girl, she heard voices persuading her 'to go and fight like a man in the service of the Dauphin.' In this scene she meets the Dauphin, the uncrowned King Charles the Seventh, in the throne room of the castle at Chinon. Joan is about 17, strong, healthy, lively, imaginative; a contrast to the Dauphin, described as 'a poor creature physically, aged 26, . . . with the expression of a young dog about to be kicked,' also 'incorrigible, irrepressible, and at present excited, like a child with a new toy.'

Time: March 1429.

The Duchess passes on. JOAN *stares after her; then whispers to the* DAUPHIN.

JOAN. Be that Queen?

CHARLES. No. She thinks she is.

JOAN (*again staring after the Duchess*). Oo-oo-ooh! (*Her awestruck amazement at the figure cut by the magnificently dressed lady is not wholly complimentary. To the* DAUPHIN.) Who be old Gruff-and-Grum?

CHARLES. He is the Duke de la Trémouille.

JOAN. What be his job?

CHARLES. He pretends to command the army. And whenever I find a friend I can care for, he kills him.

JOAN. Why dost let him?

CHARLES (*petulantly moving to the throne side of the room to escape from her magnetic field*). How can I prevent him? He bullies me. They all bully me.

JOAN. Art afraid?

CHARLES. Yes: I am afraid. It's no use preaching to me about it. It's all very well for these big men with their armor that is too heavy for me, and their swords that I can hardly lift, and their muscle and their shouting and their bad tempers. They like fighting: most of them are making fools of themselves all the time they are not fighting; but I am quiet and sensible; and I don't want to kill people: I only want to be left alone to enjoy myself in my own way. I never asked to be a king: it was pushed on me. So if you are going to say 'Son of St Louis: gird on the sword of your ancestors, and lead us to victory' you may spare your breath to cool your porridge; for I cannot do it. I am not built that way; and there is an end of it.

JOAN (*trenchant and masterful*). Blethers! We are all like that to begin with. I shall put courage into thee.

CHARLES. But I don't want to have courage put into me. I want to sleep in a comfortable bed, and not live in continual terror of being killed or wounded. Put courage into the others, and let them have their bellyful of fighting; but let me alone.

JOAN. It's no use, Charlie: thou must face what God puts on thee. If thou fail to make thyself king, thoult be a beggar: what else art fit for? Come! Let me see thee sitting on the throne. I have looked forward to that.

CHARLES. What is the good of sitting on the throne when the other fellows give all the orders? However! (*He sits enthroned, a piteous figure.*) Here is the king for you! Look your fill at the poor devil.

183

JOAN. Thourt not king yet, lad: thourt but Dauphin. Be not led away by them around thee. Dressing up don't fill empty noddle. I know the people: the real people that make thy bread for thee; and I tell thee they count no man king of France until the holy oil has been poured on his hair, and himself consecrated and crowned in Rheims Cathedral. And thou needs new clothes, Charlie. Why does not Queen look after thee properly?

CHARLES. We're too poor. She wants all the money we can spare to put on her own back. Besides, I like to see her beautifully dressed; and I dont care what I wear myself: I should look ugly anyhow.

JOAN. There is some good in thee, Charlie, but it is not yet a king's good.

CHARLES. We shall see. I am not such a fool as I look. I have my eyes open; and I can tell you that one good treaty is worth ten good fights. These fighting fellows lose all on the treaties that they gain on the fights. If we can only have a treaty, the English are sure to have the worst of it, because they are better at fighting than at thinking.

JOAN. If the English win, it is they that will make the treaty; and then God help poor France! Thou must fight, Charlie, whether thou will or no. I will go first to hearten thee. We must take our courage in both hands: aye, and pray for it with both hands too.

CHARLES (*descending from his throne and again crossing the room to escape from her dominating urgency*). Oh do stop talking about God and praying. I cant bear people who are always praying. Isnt it bad enough to have to do it at the proper times?

JOAN (*pitying him*). Thou poor child, thou hast never prayed in thy life. I must teach thee from the beginning.
184

CHARLES. I am not a child: I am a grown man and a father; and I will not be taught any more.

JOAN. Aye, you have a little son. He that will be Louis the Eleventh when you die. Would you not fight for him?

CHARLES. No: a horrid boy. He hates me. He hates everybody, selfish little beast! I dont want to be bothered with children. I dont want to be a father; and I dont want to be a son: especially a son of St Louis. I dont want to be any of these fine things you all have your heads full of: I want to be just what I am. Why cant you mind your own business, and let me mind mine?

JOAN (*again contemptuous*). Minding your own business is like minding your own body: it's the shortest way to make yourself sick. What is my business? Helping mother at home. What is thine? Petting lapdogs and sucking sugar-sticks. I call that muck. I tell thee it is God's business we are here to do: not our own. I have a message to thee from God; and thou must listen to it, though thy heart break with the terror of it.

CHARLES. I don't want a message; but can you tell me any secrets? Can you do any cares? Can you turn lead into gold, or anything of that sort?

JOAN. I can turn thee into a king, in Rheims Cathedral; and that is a miracle that will take some doing, it seems.

CHARLES. If we go to Rheims, and have a coronation, Anne will want new dresses. We cant afford them. I am all right as I am.

JOAN. As you are! And what is that? Less than my father's poorest shepherd. Thourt not lawful owner of thy own land of France till thou be consecrated.

CHARLES. But I shall not be lawful owner of my own land anyhow. Will the consecration pay off my mortgages? I have pledged my last acre to the Archbishop and that fat bully. I owe money even to Bluebeard.

JOAN (*earnestly*). Charlie: I come from the land, and have gotten my strength working on the land; and I tell thee that the land is thine to rule righteously and keep God's peace in, and not to pledge at the pawnshop as a drunken woman pledges her children's clothes. And I come from God to tell thee to kneel in the cathedral and solemnly give thy kingdom to Him for ever and ever, and become the greatest king in the world as His steward and His bailiff, His soldier and His servant. The very clay of France will become holy: her soldiers will be the soldiers of God: the rebel dukes will be rebels against God: the English will fall on their knees and beg thee let them return to their lawful homes in peace. Wilt be a poor little Judas, and betray me and Him that sent me?

CHARLES (*tempted at last*). Oh, if I only dare!

JOAN. I shall dare, dare, and dare again, in God's name! Art for or against me?

CHARLES (*excited*). I'll risk it. I warn you I shant be able to keep it up; but I'll risk it. You shall see. (*Running to the main door and shouting.*) Hallo! Come back, everybody. (*To Joan, as he runs back to the arch opposite.*) Mind you stand by and dont let me be bullied.

A Trip To Scarborough
Richard Brinsley Sheridan

Colonel Townley, relinquishing his love for the sprightly widow Berinthia, now has designs on Amanda, wife of Loveless, who in turn – believed by his young wife to be as faithful as she is herself – is attracted to Berinthia. Amanda is lively, playful and demure; Berinthia, a woman of the world, sophisticated and scheming. The scene takes place at Loveless's lodgings in Scarborough, Yorkshire.

Time: 1781.

AMANDA. I'm glad to find he does not like her, for I have a great mind to persuade her to come and live with me. (*Aside.*)

BERINTHIA. So! I find my colonel continues in his airs: there must be something more at the bottom of this than the provocation he pretends from me. (*Aside.*)

AMANDA. For Heaven's sake, Berinthia, tell me what way I shall take to persuade you to come and live with me.

BERINTHIA. Why, one way in the world there is, and but one.

AMANDA. And pray what is that?

BERINTHIA. It is to assure me – I shall be very welcome.

BERINTHIA. If that be all, you shall e'en sleep here to-night.

BERINTHIA. To-night!

AMANDA. Yes, to-night.

BERINTHIA. Why, the people where I lodge will think me mad.

AMANDA. Let 'em think what they please.

BERINTHIA. Say you so, Amanda? Why, then, they shall think what they please: for I'm a young widow, and I care not what anybody thinks. – Ah, Amanda, it's a delicious thing to be a young widow!

AMANDA. You'll hardly make me think so.

BERINTHIA. Puh! because you are in love with your husband – but that is not every woman's case.

AMANDA. I hope 'twas yours at least.

BERINTHIA. Mine, say you? – Now I have a great mind to tell you a lie, but I shall do it so awkwardly, you'll find me out.

AMANDA. Then e'en speak the truth.

BERINTHIA. Shall I? – then, after all, I did love him, Amanda, as a Nun does penance.

AMANDA. How did you live together?

BERINTHIA. Like man and wife – asunder – he lov'd the country – I the town. – He hawks and hounds – I coaches and equipage. – He eating and drinking – I carding and playing. – He the sound of a horn – I the squeak of a fiddle. – We were dull company at table – worse a-bed: whenever we met we gave one another the spleen, and never agreed but once, which was about lying alone.

AMANDA. But tell me one thing truly and sincerely – notwithstanding all these jars, did not his death at last extremely trouble you?

BERINTHIA. O yes. – I was forced to wear an odious Widow's band a twelve-month for't.

AMANDA. Women, I find, have different inclinations: – prithee, Berinthia, instruct me a little farther – for I'm so great a novice, I'm almost ashamed on't. – Not Heav'n knows that what you call intrigues have any charms for me – the practical part of all unlawful love is –

BERINTHIA. O 'tis abominable – but for the speculative, that we must all confess is entertaining enough.

AMANDA. Pray, be so just then to me, to believe, 'tis with a world of innocence I would inquire whether you think those we call women of reputation do really escape all other men as they do those shadows of beaux?

BERINTHIA. Oh, no, Amanda; there are a sort of men make dreadful work amongst 'em, men that may be called the beau's antipathy, for they agree in nothing but walking upon two legs. These have brains, the beau has none. These are in love with their mistress, the beau with himself. They take care of their reputation, he's industrious to destroy it. They are decent, he's a fop; in short, they are men, he's an ass.

AMANDA. If this be their character, I fancy we had here, e'en now, a pattern of 'em both.

BERINTHIA. His lordship and Colonel Townly?

AMANDA. The same.

BERINTHIA. As for the lord, he is eminently so; and for the other, I can assure you there's not a man in town who has a better interest with the women that are worth having an interest with.

AMANDA. He answers then the opinion I had ever of him. – Heavens! what a difference there is between a man like him, and that vain nauseous fop, Lord Foppington (*Taking her hand.*) I must acquaint you with a secret, cousin – 'tis not

189

that fool alone has talked to me of love; Townly has been tampering too.

BERINTHIA (*Aside*). So, so! here the mystery comes out! – Colonel Townly! impossible, my dear!

AMANDA. 'Tis true, indeed; though he has done it in vain; nor do I think that all the merit of mankind combined could shake the tender love I bear my husband; yet I will own to you, Berinthia, I did not start at his addresses, as when they came from one whom I contemned.

BERINTHIA (*Aside*). Oh, this is better and better! – Well said, Innocence! and you really think, my dear, that nothing could abate your constancy and attachment to your husband?

AMANDA. Nothing, I am convinced.

BERINTHIA. What, if you found he loved another woman better?

AMANDA. Well!

BERINTHIA. Well! – why, were I that thing they call a slighted wife, somebody should run the risk of being that thing they call – a husband.

AMANDA. O fie, Berinthia, no revenge should ever be taken against a husband – but to wrong his bed is a vengeance, which of all vengeance –

BERINTHIA. Is the sweetest! – ha! ha! ha! – don't I talk madly?

AMANDA. Madly, indeed!

BERINTHIA. Yet I'm very innocent.

AMANDA. That I dare swear you are. I know how to make allowance for your humour: but you resolve, then, never to marry again?

BERINTHIA. Oh, no! I resolve I will.

AMANDA. How so?

BERINTHIA. That I never may.

AMANDA. You banter me.

BERINTHIA. Indeed I don't: but I consider I'm a woman, and form my resolutions accordingly.

AMANDA. Well, my opinion is, form what resolutions you will, matrimony will be the end on't.

BERINTHIA. I doubt it – but a – Heavens! I have business at home, and am half an hour too late.

AMANDA. As you are to return with me, I'll just give some orders, and walk with you.

BERINTHIA. Well, make haste, and we'll finish this subject as we go. – (*Exit* AMANDA.) Ah, poor Amanda! you have led a country life. Well, this discovery is lucky! Base Townly! at once false to me and treacherous to his friend! – And my innocent, demure cousin too! I have it in my power to be revenged on her, however. Her husband, if I have any skill in countenance, would be as happy in my smiles as Townly can hope to be in hers. I'll make the experiment, come what will on't. The woman who can forgive the being robbed of a favoured lover must be either an idiot or a wanton.

Journey's End
R C Sheriff

Captain Stanhope, a good-looking young man, is suffering from excessive alcohol and the strains of war. At 21, he is three years older than Lieutenant Raleigh, a well-built healthy boy, new to war, who had previously worshipped Stanhope at their public school. Raleigh is anxious to do the right thing and please everyone, but the situation between the two men becomes uneasy. They are in a dug-out in the British trenches before St Quentin, France.

Time: March 20th, 1918.

RALEIGH *comes slowly down the steps. He pauses at the bottom, takes off his helmet, and hesitates.* STANHOPE *is sitting at the table puffing at the remains of his cigar. There is silence except for the rumble of the guns.*

STANHOPE. I thought I told you to come down to dinner at eight o'clock?

RALEIGH. Oh, I'm sorry. I didn't think you – er –

STANHOPE. Well? You didn't think I – er – what?

RALEIGH. I didn't think you'd – you'd mind – if I didn't.

STANHOPE. I see. And why do you think I asked you – if I didn't mind?

RALEIGH. I'm sorry.

STANHOPE. Well, we've kept your dinner. It's ready for you here.

RALEIGH. Oh, it's awfully good of you to have kept it for me, but – I – I had something to eat up there.

192

STANHOPE. You – had something to eat up there? What do you mean, exactly?

RALEIGH. They brought the tea round while I was on duty. I had a cup, and some bread and cheese.

STANHOPE. Are you telling me – you've been feeding with the men?

RALEIGH. Well, Sergeant Baker suggested –

STANHOPE. So you take your orders from Sergeant Baker, do you?

RALEIGH. No, but –

STANHOPE. You eat the men's rations when there's barely enough for each man?

RALEIGH. They asked me to share.

STANHOPE. Now, look here. I know you're new to this, but I thought you'd have the common sense to leave the men alone to their meals. Do you think they want an officer prowling round eating their rations, and sucking up to them like that? My officers are here to be respected – not laughed at.

RALEIGH. Why did they ask me – if they didn't mean it?

STANHOPE. Don't you realize they were making a fool of you?

RALEIGH. Why should they?

STANHOPE. So you know more about my men than I do? (*There is silence.* RALEIGH *is facing* STANHOPE *squarely.*)

RALEIGH. I'm sorry then – if I was wrong.

STANHOPE. Sit down.

RALEIGH. It's all right, thanks.

193

STANHOPE (*suddenly shouting*). *Sit down!* (RALEIGH *sits on the box to the right of the table.* STANHOPE *speaks quietly again.*) I understand you prefer being up there with the men than down here with us?

RALEIGH. I don't see what you mean.

STANHOPE. What did you tell Hibbert?

RALEIGH. Hibbert? I – I didn't say –

STANHOPE. Don't lie.

RALEIGH (*rising*). I'm not lying! Why should I – lie?

STANHOPE. Then why didn't you come down to supper when I told you to?

RALEIGH. I – I wasn't hungry. I had rather a headache. It's cooler up there.

STANHOPE. You insulted Trotter and Hibbert by not coming. You realize that, I suppose?

RALEIGH. I didn't mean to do anything like that.

STANHOPE. Well, you did. You know now – don't you? (RALEIGH *makes no reply. He is trying to understand why* STANHOPE'*s temper has risen to a trembling fury.* STAN-HOPE *can scarcely control his voice. Loudly.*) I say – you *know* now don't you?

RALEIGH. Yes, I'm sorry.

STANHOPE. My officers work *together*. I'll have no damn prigs.

RALEIGH. I'll speak to Trotter and Hibbert. I didn't realize – (STANHOPE *raises his cigar. His hand trembles so violently that he can scarcely take the cigar between his teeth.* RALEIGH *looks at* STANHOPE, *fascinated and horrified.*)

STANHOPE. What are you looking at?

194

RALEIGH (*lowering his head*). Nothing.

STANHOPE. Anything – *funny* about me?

RALEIGH. No. (*After a moment's silence, RALEIGH speaks in a low, halting voice.*) I'm awfully sorry, Dennis, if – if I annoyed you by coming to your company.

STANHOPE. What on *earth* are you talking about? What do you mean?

RALEIGH. You resent my being here.

STANHOPE. Resent you *being* here?

RALEIGH. Ever since I came –

STANHOPE. I don't know what you mean. I resent you being a damn fool, that's all. (*There is a pause.*) Better eat your dinner before it's cold.

RALEIGH. I'm not hungry, thanks.

STANHOPE. Oh, for God's sake, sit down and eat it like a man!

RALEIGH. I can't eat it, thanks.

STANHOPE (*shouting*). Are you going to eat your dinner?

RALEIGH. Good God! Don't you understand? How *can* I sit down and eat that – when – (*His voice is nearly breaking.*) when Osborne's – lying – out there – (STANHOPE *rises slowly. His eyes are wild and staring; he is fighting for breath, and his words come brokenly.*)

STANHOPE. My God! You bloody little swine! You think I don't care – you think you're the only soul that cares!

RALEIGH. And yet you can sit there and drink champagne – and smoke cigars –

195

STANHOPE. The one man I could trust – my best friend – the one man I could talk to as man to man – who understood everything – and you think I don't care –

RALEIGH. But how can you when – ?

STANHOPE. To forget, you little fool – to forget! D'you understand? To forget! You think there's no limit to what a man can bear? (*He turns quickly from* RALEIGH *and goes to the dark corner by* OSBORNE'*s bed. He stands with his face towards the wall, his shoulders heaving as he fights for breath.*)

RALEIGH. I'm awfully sorry, Dennis. I – I didn't understand. (STANHOPE *makes no reply.*) You don't know how – I –

STANHOPE. Go away, please – leave me alone.

RALEIGH. Can't I – (STANHOPE *turns wildly upon* RALEIGH.)

STANHOPE. Oh, get out! For God's sake, get out! (RALEIGH *goes away into his dug-out, and* STANHOPE *is alone. The Very lights rise and fall outside, softly breaking the darkness with their glow – sometimes steel-blue, sometimes grey. Through the night there comes the impatient grumble of gunfire that never dies away.*)

Rutherford and Son
Githa Sowerby

John Rutherford is 'The Master' (this play's original title) of his Works as well as his own family, dominating all they do. He disapproves of his son John's marriage to a London office worker, Mary, but the couple (with their baby son) have now come to live in the bleak, Northern family home with Rutherford, his sister Ann and unmarried daughter, Janet. Ann is a faded, querulous, rather narrow-minded woman of about 60, wearing black with a ribboned cap. She sits knitting by the living-room fire with Mary, aged 26, gentle and delicate-looking, who is sewing. . . .
    Time: 1912.

ANN. Eh, dearie – dearie. Sic doings!

MARY (*absorbed in her cap*). Never mind, Miss Rutherford.

ANN. Never mind! It's well for you to talk.

MARY. Janet'll see that it's all right. She always does, though she talks like that.

ANN. Her and her sulky ways. There's no doing anything with her of late. She used to be bad enough as a lass, that passionate and hard to drive. She's ten times worse now she's turned quiet.

MARY. Perhaps she's tired with the long walks she takes. She's been out nearly two hours this afternoon in the rain.

ANN (*turning to her knitting*). What should she have to put her out – except her own tempers.

MARY (*trying to divert her attention*). Miss Rutherford, look at Tony's cap; I've nearly finished it.

197

ANN (*still cross*). It's weel enough. Though what he wants wi' a lot o' bows standing up all over his head passes me.

MARY. They're butterfly bows.

ANN. Butterfly bows! And what'll butterfly bows do for 'n? They'll no keep his head warm.

MARY. But he looks such a darling in them. I'll put it on tomorrow when I take him out, and you'll see.

ANN. London ways – that's what it is.

MARY. Do north-country babies never have bows on their caps?

ANN. Not in these parts. And not the Rutherfords anyway. Plain and lasting – that's the rule in this family, and we bide by it, babies and all. But you can't be expected to know, and you like a stranger in the hoose.

MARY (*who has gone to the window and is looking out at the winter twilight*). If I'm a stranger, it's you that makes me so.

ANN. Ye've no cause to speak so, lass. . . . I'm not blamin' you. It's no' your fault that you weren't born and bred in the north country.

MARY. No. I can't change that. . . . I wonder what it's like here when the sun shines!

ANN. Sun?

MARY. It doesn't look as if the summer ever came here.

ANN. If ye're looking for the summer in the middle o' December ye'll no' get it. Ye'll soon get used to it. Ye've happened on a bad autumn for your first, that's all.

MARY. My first.

ANN. Ye're a bit saft wi' livin' in the sooth, nae doubt. They tell me there's a deal of sunshine and wickedness in them parts.

MARY. The people are happier, I think.

ANN. Mebbees. Bein' happy'll make no porridge.

MARY. I lived in Devonshire when I was a child, and everywhere there were lanes. But here – it's all so old and stern – this great stretch of moor, and the fells – and the trees – all bent one way, crooked and huddled.

ANN (*absorbed in her knitting*). It's the sea-wind that does it.

MARY. The one that's blowing now?

ANN. Aye.

MARY (*with a shiver*). Shall I draw the curtains.

ANN. Aye. (MARY *draws the curtains. After a silence she speaks again gently.*)

MARY. I wonder if you'll ever get used to me enough to – like me?

ANN (*with the north-country dislike of anything demonstrative*). Like you! Sic a question – and you a kind of a relation.

MARY. Myself, I mean.

ANN. You're weel enough. You're a bit slip of a thing, but you're John's wife, and the mother of his bairn, and there's an end.

MARY. Yes, that's all I am! (*She takes up her work again.*)

ANN. Now you're talking.

MARY (*sewing*). Don't think I don't understand. John and I have been married five years. All that time Mr Rutherford never once asked to see me; if I had died, he would have been glad.

ANN. I don't say that. He's a proud man, and he looked higher for his son after the eddication he'd given him. You mustn't be thinking such things.

MARY (*without bitterness*). Oh, I know all about it. If I hadn't been Tony's mother, he would never have had me inside his house. And if I hadn't been Tony's mother, I wouldn't have come. Not for anything in the world. . . . It's wonderful how he's picked up since he got out of those stuffy lodgings.

ANN (*winding up her wool*). Well, Mr Rutherford's in the right after all.

MARY. Oh yes. He's in the right.

ANN. It's a bitter thing for him that's worked all his life to make a place i' the world to have his son go off and marry secret-like. Folk like him look for a return from their bairns. It's weel known that no good comes of a marriage such as yours, and it's no wonder that it takes him a bit of time to make up his mind to bide it. (*Getting up to go.*) But what's done's done.

Home
David Storey

Kathleen is a stout lady in older middle-age, wearing an unbuttoned coat, a head-scarf and strap shoes. She is limping, her arm supported by Marjorie, who is of similar age dressed in skirt and cardigan, and carrying an umbrella and a well-used bag. They are residents in a mental home and are outside the building where a round metal-work table and two chairs are placed.
  Time: The present.

KATHLEEN. Cor . . . *blimey!*

MARJORIE. Going to rain, ask me.

KATHLEEN. Rain all it wants, ask me. Cor . . . *blimey!* Going to kill me is this. (*Limps to a chair, sits down and holds her foot.*)

MARJORIE. Going to rain and catch us out here. That's what it's going to do. (*Puts umbrella up; worn, but not excessively so.*)

KATHLEEN. Going to rain all right, i'n't it? Going to rain all right . . . Put your umbrella up – sun's still shining. Cor blimey. Invite rain that will. Commonsense, girl . . . Cor *blimey* . . . My bleedin' feet . . . (*Rubs one foot without removing shoe.*)

MARJORIE. Out here and no shelter. Be all right if it starts. (*Moves umbrella one way then another, looking up.*)

KATHLEEN. Cor *blimey* . . . 'Surprise me they don't drop off . . . Cut clean through, these will.

201

MARJORIE (*looking skywards, however*). Clouds all over. Told you we shouldn't have come out.

KATHLEEN. Get nothing if you don't try, girl . . . Cor *blimey!* (*Winces.*)

MARJORIE. I don't know.

KATHLEEN. Here. You'll be all right, won't you?

MARJORIE. . . . ?

KATHLEEN. Holes there is. See right through, you can.

MARJORIE. What?

KATHLEEN. Here. Rain come straight through that. Won't get much shelter under that. What d'I tell you? Might as well sit under a shower. (*Laughs.*) Cor blimey. You'll be all right, won't you?

MARJORIE. Be all right with you in any case. Walk no faster than a snail.

MARJORIE. Not surprised. Don't want me to escape. That's my trouble, girl.

MARJORIE. Here . . . (*Sits.* JACK *and* HARRY *slowly pass upstage, taking the air, chatting.* MARJORIE *and* KATHLEEN *wait for them to pass.*)

KATHLEEN. What've we got for lunch?

MARJORIE. Sprouts.

KATHLEEN (*massaging foot*). Seen them, have you?

MARJORIE. Smelled 'em!

KATHLEEN. What's today, then?

MARJORIE. Friday.

KATHLEEN. End of week.

MARJORIE. Corn' beef hash.

MARJORIE. That's Wednesday.

KATHLEEN. Sausage roll.

MARJORIE. Think you're right . . . Cor *blimey*. (*Groans, holding her foot.*)

MARJORIE. Know what you ought to do, don't you? (KATHLEEN *groans holding her foot.*) Ask for another pair of shoes, girl, you ask me.

MARJORIE. Took me laced ones, haven't they? Only ones that fitted. Thought I'd hang myself, didn't they? Only five inches long.

MARJORIE. What they think you are?

KATHLEEN. Bleedin' mouse, more likely.

MARJORIE. Here. Not like the last one I was in.

KATHLEEN. No?

MARJORIE. Let you paint on the walls, they did. Do anyfing. Just muck around . . . Here . . . I won't tell you what some of them did.

KATHLEEN. What? (MARJORIE *leans over, whispers.*) Never.

MARJORIE. Cross me heart.

KATHLEEN. Glad I wasn't there. This place is bad enough. You seen Henderson, have you?

MARJORIE. Ought to lock him up, you ask me.

KATHLEEN. What d'you do, then?

MARJORIE. Here?

KATHLEEN. At this other place.

MARJORIE. Noffing. Mucked around . . .

KATHLEEN. Here . . . (JACK *and* HARRY *stroll back again, slowly, upstage, in conversation; head back, deep breathing, bracing arms . . .* MARJORIE *and* KATHLEEN *wait till they pass.*)

MARJORIE. My dentist comes from Pakistan.

KATHLEEN. Yours?

MARJORIE. Took out all me teeth.

KATHLEEN. Those not your own, then?

MARJORIE. All went rotten when I had my little girl. There she is, waitress at the seaside.

KATHLEEN. And you stuck here . . .

MARJORIE. No teeth . . .

KATHLEEN. Don't appreciate it.

MARJORIE. They don't.

KATHLEEN. Never.

MARJORIE. Might take this down if it doesn't rain.

KATHLEEN. Cor blimey . . . take these off if I thought I could get 'em on again . . . (*Groans.*) Tried catching a serious disease.

MARJORIE. When was that?

KATHLEEN. Only had me in two days. Said, nothing the matter with you, my girl.

MARJORIE. Don't believe you.

KATHLEEN. Next thing: got home; smashed everything in sight.

MARJORIE. No?

204

KATHLEEN. Winders. Cooker . . . Nearly broke me back . . . Thought I'd save the telly. Still owed eighteen months. Thought: 'Everything or nothing, girl.'

MARJORIE. Rotten programmes. (*Takes down umbrella.*)

KATHLEEN. Didn't half give it a good old conk.

MARJORIE (*looking round*). There's one thing. You get a good night's sleep.

KATHLEEN. Like being with a steam engine, where I come from. Cor blimey, that much whistling and groaning; think you're going to take off.

MARJORIE. More like a boa constrictor, ask me. Here . . . (JACK *and* HARRY *stroll back, still taking the air, upstage; bracing, head back . . .*) Started crying everywhere I went . . . Started off on Christmas Eve.

KATHLEEN. 'S'happy time, Christmas.

MARJORIE. Didn't stop till Boxing Day.

KATHLEEN. If He ever comes again I hope He comes on Whit Tuesday. For me that's the best time of the year.

MARJORIE. Why's that?

KATHLEEN. Dunno. Whit Tuesday's always been a lucky day for me. First party I ever went to was on a Whit Tuesday. First feller I went with. Can't be the date. Different every year.

MARJORIE. My lucky day's the last Friday in any month with an 'r' in it when the next month doesn't begin later than the following Monday.

KATHLEEN. How do you make that out?

MARJORIE. Dunno. I was telling the doctor that the other day . . . There's that man with the binoculars watching you.

KATHLEEN. Where?

MARJORIE. Lift your dress up.

KATHLEEN. No.

MARJORIE. Go on . . . (*Leans over; does it for her.*) Told you . . .

KATHLEEN. Looks like he's got diarrhoea! (*They laugh.*) See that chap the other day? Showed his slides of a trip up the Amazon River.

MARJORIE. See that one with no clothes on? Supposed to be cooking his dinner.

KATHLEEN. Won't have him here again . . .

MARJORIE. Showing all his ps and qs.

KATHLEEN. Oooooh! (*Laughs, covering her mouth.*)

MARJORIE. Here . . . (*Glances after* JACK *and* HARRY *as they stroll off.*) See that woman with dyed hair? Told me she'd been in films. 'What films?' I said. 'Blue films?'

KATHLEEN. What she say?

MARJORIE. 'The ones I was in was not in colour.' (*They laugh.*) I s'll lose me teeth one of these days . . . oooh!

KATHLEEN. Better'n losing something else . . .

MARJORIE. Oooooh! (*They laugh again.*)

KATHLEEN. Here . . .

Spring Awakening
Frank Wedekind

Subtitled A Children's Tragedy, *the play deals with mishandled authority, the veiling of truth, the repression of adolescent growth and freedom. Frau Bergmann is the stereotypical bourgeois mother, anxious to keep her daughter a child; while Wendla, at 14, on the threshold of growing up, is equally anxious to learn more of love and life. They are in the living-room of the Bergmanns' house in a provincial town in Germany.*

Time: 1891.

FRAU BERGMANN *wearing a hat and cape, and with a beaming face, comes through the middle door. She carries a basket on her arm.*

FRAU BERGMANN. Wendla! Wendla! (WENDLA *appears in petticoat and stays at the side door right.*)

WENDLA. What is it, mother?

FRAU BERGMANN. You're up already, precious? What a good girl!

WENDLA. You've been out this early?

FRAU BERGMANN. Get dressed quickly. You must go down to Ina. You must take her this basket.

WENDLA (*gets fully dressed during the following*). You've been to Ina's? How was Ina? Won't she ever get better?

FRAU BERGMANN. You'll never guess, Wendla, last night the stork was with her and brought her a little boy.

WENDLA. A boy! A boy! O that's wonderful! That's what her chronic influenza was!

FRAU BERGMANN. A perfect boy!

WENDLA. I must see him, mother! Now I'm an aunt three times – aunt to one girl and two boys!

FRAU BERGMANN. And what boys! That's what happens when you live so close to the stork! It's only two years since she walked up the aisle in her white dress.

WENDLA. Were you there when he brought him?

FRAU BERGMANN. He'd just flown off again. Don't you want to pin on a rose?

WENDLA. Why didn't you get there a bit sooner, mother?

FRAU BERGMANN. I believe he might have brought you something too – a brooch perhaps.

WENDLA. It's such a pity.

FRAU BERGMANN. Now I told you he brought you a brooch.

WENDLA. I've got enough brooches.

FRAU BERGMANN. Then be contented, child. What more do you want?

WENDLA. I would very much like to have known whether he flew in through the window or down the chimney.

FRAU BERGMANN. You must ask Ina. O yes, you must ask Ina that, precious. Ina will tell you exactly. Ina spoke to him for a good half hour.

WENDLA. I shall ask Ina when I get there.

FRAU BERGMANN. And don't forget, precious. I shall be very interested myself to know if he came in through the window or the chimney.

WENDLA. Or perhaps I'd better ask the chimney-sweep. The chimney-sweep's bound to know if he used the chimney.

FRAU BERGMANN. Not the chimney-sweep, dear. Not the chimney-sweep. What does the chimney-sweep know about storks? He'll tell you all sorts of nonsense he doesn't believe himself. What – what are you staring at in the street?

WENDLA. Mother, a man – as big as three horses, with feet like paddle-steamers!

FRAU BERGMANN (*running to the window*). I don't believe it! I don't believe it!

WENDLA (*at the same time*). He's holding a bed-stead under his chin and playing 'Watch on the Rhine' on it – he's just gone round the corner.

FRAU BERGMANN. You'll always be a child! Frightening your silly old mother. Go and get your hat. I sometimes wonder if you'll ever get any sense in your head. I've given up hope.

WENDLA. So have I, mother, so have I. There's not much hope for my head. I've got a sister who's been married two and a half years, and I'm an aunt three times, and I've no idea how it all happens . . . Don't be cross, mummy, don't be cross! Who in the world should I ask but you? Please, mummy, tell me. Tell me, dear. I feel ashamed of myself. Do tell me, mummy! Don't scold me for asking such things. Answer me – what is it? – how does it happen? You can't really insist that now I'm fourteen I still have to believe in the stork?

FRAU BERGMANN. But good lord, child, how funny you are! What ideas you get! I really cannot do such a thing.

WENDLA. Why not, mother? Why not? It can't be anything ugly if it makes you all so happy.

FRAU BERGMANN. O – O God help me! I would deserve to be . . . Go and get dressed, Wendla. Get dressed.

WENDLA. I'll go . . . and what if your child goes to the chimney-sweep to ask?

FRAU BERGMANN. But this will send me out of my mind! Come here, Wendla, come to me. I'll tell you! I'll tell you everything! O Almighty Father! – Only not now, Wendla. Tomorrow, the day after tomorrow, next week – whenever you like, my precious.

WENDLA. Tell me today, mother! Tell me now! This moment. I can never stop asking now I've seen you so frightened.

FRAU BERGMANN. I can't Wendla.

WENDLA. O why can't you, mummy? I'll kneel at your feet and lay my head in your lap. Put your apron over my head and talk and talk as if you were sitting alone in your room. I won't flinch or cry out. I'll be patient and bear it whatever it is.

FRAU BERGMANN. Heaven knows none of this is my fault. Wendla! Heaven sees into my heart. I'll put myself into God's hands, Wendla – and tell you how you came into this world. Now listen to me, Wendla.

WENDLA (*under the apron*). I'm listening.

FRAU BERGMANN (*ecstatically*). But I can't, child! I can't be responsible! I'd deserve to be put in prison – to have you taken away from me . . .

WENDLA (*under the apron*). Be brave, mother!

FRAU BERGMANN. Well, listen!

WENDLA (*under the apron, trembling*). O God, o God!

FRAU BERGMANN. To have a child – you understand me, Wendla?

WENDLA. Quickly, mother – I can't bear it anymore.

FRAU BERGMANN. To have a child – the man – to whom you're married – you must – *love* – love, you see – as you can only love your husband. You must love him *very much with your whole heart* – in a way that can't be put into words! You must *love* him, Wendla, in a way that you certainly can't love at your age . . . Now you know.

WENDLA (*getting up*). Well, good heavens!

FRAU BERGMANN. Now you know what a testing time lies before you!

WENDLA And that's all?

FRAU BERGMANN. As God is my witness! Now take that basket and go to Ina. She'll give you some chocolate to drink, and some cake too. Come on, let me look at you once more – boots laced up, silk gloves, sailor suit, rose in your hair . . . your little skirt really is getting too short for you, Wendla!

WENDLA. Have you bought the meat for lunch, mummy?

FRAU BERGMANN. God bless you. I must sew a broad flounce round the bottom.

Frost in May
Antonia White

Nanda, 13, has been a pupil at a Roman Catholic Convent, Lippington, for four years. She is settled into the regime of the place and well-versed in Christian doctrine. She forms a romantic attachment to the beautiful Clare Rockingham, who is 17 and attracted to Catholicism against the wishes of her wealthy Protestant family. She has borrowed Nanda's rosary.

Time: 1930s.

CLARE (*sees that* NANDA *has a doubtful look, and tweaks her pigtail*). What is it, baby? Will it hurt your rosary to be used by a pagan?

NANDA. I'll have to get it blessed again, that's all.

CLARE. I say, am I as wicked as all that? Do I actually put a curse on everything I touch?

NANDA. Of course not. I'd have to get it blessed again if I lent it to anyone . . . even the Pope himself. You see, a rosary's only blessed for the person it belongs to, and so if anyone else uses it they don't get the indulgences and you don't either until it's been blessed again. Mine's blessed for a happy death, so I mustn't forget to have it done.

CLARE. What a fantastic idea, darling. Does it cost anything, having your beads blessed?

NANDA (*profoundly shocked*). Of course not.

CLARE. Don't look so hurt, baby. I'm only a poor, inquiring heathen. But I always thought there was something called a sale of indulgences.

NANDA (*kindly*). Lots of Protestants think so. But it's quite untrue. They think that three hundred days' indulgence means that you get three hundred days off purgatory. But of course, that's quite impossible, because there isn't any time in purgatory.

CLARE. Well, what does it mean then?

NANDA. It's rather a long explanation.

CLARE. Go on, I'm fascinated.

NANDA. Well, it's like this. To begin with, every mortal sin has two sorts of punishment, temporal and eternal. If you die in mortal sin, you go straight to hell. But you're let off the eternal punishment if you confess your sin and get absolution.

CLARE. Then I should just go on sinning and being forgiven as often as I liked.

NANDA (*hastily*). Oh, no, because part of the condition of getting absolution at all is that you have to have a sincere intention not to commit the sin again.

CLARE (*thinking about this*). I see. By the way, how do I know when it IS a mortal sin?

NANDA. That's awfully easy. There's got to be grave matter, full knowledge and full consent. So if you kill someone by accident, it isn't a mortal sin. Unless you mean to hurt them badly, when of course it would be. Then take stealing. It's rather difficult to know just how much would constitute grave matter. But it's generally supposed to be about half a crown.

CLARE. So if I stole two and fivepence, it would only be a venial sin?

NANDA (*a little doubtful*). Ye-es. But, of course, if two and fivepence was all the person had, or if they were a widow or

213

an orphan, or if you stole it from a church box, it would be mortal.

CLARE. And suppose it was a very dark night and I meant to steal a half-crown and it turned out to be two shillings, it would only be a venial sin?

NANDA (*positively*). Good gracious, no. It would be a mortal sin because you had the *intention* of stealing half a crown.

CLARE. You Catholics are wonderfully definite about everything, aren't you? It must be a great comfort to know just where one is. But go on about indulgences.

NANDA. Sure I'm not boring you?

CLARE. Not a bit, infant.

NANDA. Well, you're quite clear about eternal punishment and temporal punishment, aren't you? After the eternal punishment of a mortal sin has been remitted in confession, there's still the temporal punishment to be worked off in this life or in purgatory. Venial sins carry some temporal punishment, too, but not so much.

CLARE. I suppose there are heaps of venial sins?

NANDA (*gloomily*). Hundreds. Almost everything's a venial sin, in fact. If I don't eat my cabbage, or if I have an extra helping of pudding when I'm not really hungry, or if I think my hair looks rather nice when it's just been washed . . . they're all venial sins. And then as if one's own sins weren't enough, there are nine ways in which you can share in another person's.

CLARE. Good Lord, I bet you a holy picture you don't know 'em all.

NANDA (*shutting her eyes and gabbling*). By counsel, by command, by consent, by provocation, by praise or flattery, by being a partner in the sin by silence, by defending the ill-done.

CLARE. It's amazing. How can all you babes reel them off like that?

NANDA. Well, I've done Catechism and Christian Doctrine for two hours a day for three years.

CLARE. Then tell me something. I was reading Rosario's catechism on Sunday and I came across something very peculiar. It was one of the commandments . . . 'Thou shalt not commit adultery' and it said it forbade fornication and all wilful pleasures in the irregular motions of the flesh. What does it mean?

NANDA (*coldly*). I haven't the faintest idea. We don't do the sixth and ninth commandments. Mother Percival says they're not necessary for children. They're about some very disgusting sins, I believe, that only grown-up people commit. (CLARE *laughs, rather wildly.*) I think we'd better be getting back to the others. I promised Leo to play tennis. And, besides, we're not really supposed to be about in twos.

CLARE. Nonsense, baby. Mother Percival has got us well in the tail of her stony eye. And besides, you may be converting me, who knows?

NANDA (*assertive, but a little hurt*). I shouldn't dream of trying, Clare. Catholics don't try and convert people like that. They just answer your questions and . . . and . . . pray for you.

CLARE (*touching* NANDA's *arm, leaning closer to her*). Do you pray for me, baby?

NANDA (*blushing, but matter of fact*). Of course.

CLARE (*laughingly*). Go on about indulgences, infant theologian?

NANDA. Listen . . . Listen, Clare . . . Come on, come on quick . . . It's *deo gratias*, the holiday bell. (*She seizes CLARE's hand and they run off.*)

Effie's Burning
Valerie Windsor

Effie – short for 'that effing brat' – was committed to mental hospital as a moral defective at the age of 12, and then pushed out into 'the community' in her sixties. Despite her age, and her face, arms and hands being severely affected by recent burning, Effie retains an untouched, childlike quality. Dr Ruth Kovacs is given Effie's case by her pompous senior consultant, and as she grows closer to her patient, discovers both her own anger and courage for the future.

The women are in Effie's hospital room.
Time: The present

DR KOVACS. Good morning. Sleep well?

EFFIE. No.

DR KOVACS. No, nor did I.

EFFIE. Bad dreams. Keep remembering things. Police come again.

DR KOVACS. Did they? What did they say?

EFFIE. There's going to be a hearing, Miss. About the fire.

DR KOVACS (*about EFFIE's face which she is examining*). That looks all right.

EFFIE. No, it don't. Seen it in a mirror, Miss.

DR KOVACS. It'll look better when it's healed. By the way, I rang up Crampton Court yesterday. I asked them about your friend Alice.

EFFIE (*suddenly alert*). Alice? Where's she gone to?

217

DR KOVACS. They said she'd been transferred to The Laurels. (EFFIE *thinks hard*.) So you were both transferred to the Laurels? She was with you?

EFFIE (*after some more thought*). Stupid name. Weren't no Laurels. Weren't no nothing. Little spitty bit of a garden. They said 'Effie, we're going to close Somerville Ward.' I said 'Close it? You can't close it.' I didn't know what they meant. (*A pause. Then a slow smile*.) I chose the curtains, Miss. Yellow ones. They said 'Effie, we're going to have new curtains on Somerville. What colour would you like?' and I said – yellow.

It was safe there. We had the tele. I knew everybody. All the staff. Everybody. 'Hello, Effie.' 'Morning, Eff. You all right today, Eff?'

Me and Alice we had such good times. You could walk in the gardens if you wanted. You could sit there if it was warm. Watch everything.

'How can you close it?' I said.

'It's all right, Effie. It's going to be all right. You're going to have a room all your own . . .'

I got my own room. This is my room. My bed. Alice's bed. Dot's bed. Yellow curtains.

DR KOVACS. Careful with your arm.

EFFIE. They wanted it, Miss. Not me. I would of chose to stay, but no, we all had to go whether we wanted to or not. And they kept saying: 'Ent you lucky? Ent you a lucky girl, Eff?' And then this van come just like we was going to Weston for the day and we all had to get in. And me and Alice, we sat like this. (*Demonstrating their degree of apprehensive tension*.) 'Going to take you to see your new house, Effie. You'll like that.' 'No, I won't.' 'Yes, you will. Do what you want now.' Course, 't'was a lie. 'Cos what I wanted to do was go back home. To Somerville. But I couldn't do that, could I?

You don't know where's she's gone then, Miss?

DR KOVACS. I don't know where she is now. I'll do some more investigating for you, if you want.

EFFIE. And you tell that policeman I didn't have no matches.

DR KOVACS (*carefully*). Effie, when they came for you in the van . . . ?

EFFIE. Me and Alice, Miss, we sat like this.

DR KOVACS. No, not that time. The first time. When you were in the cupboard.

EFFIE. And my mum watching. Face like stone.

DR KOVACS. That time. Why did they come? What had you done?

EFFIE (*confused pain*). I don't know, Miss. (*A pause.*) See . . . (*Then changing her mind.*) No, no, I can't. Could've been a dream. I don't know. (DR KOVACS *says nothing, but waits.*) I can't. (*A pause.*) See, one time I was crawling in the hedges cos I was looking where this hen we had was laying. She was off by herself, see, in the hedges. So this man . . . he come down the lane . . . he saw me and what he done he pushed me through t'other side into Longacre and he done it to me. (*A long pause.*)

DR KOVACS. Did you know the man?

EFFIE. No. I seen him before but I didn't know his name.

DR KOVACS. Did you tell anyone?

EFFIE. No.

DR KOVACS. How old were you?

EFFIE. Don't know. Eleven. Twelve. Didn't know what he was going to do at first. Thought he was going to kill me, see, when he was so rough pushing me through the hedge. Every time he saw me he done it. Then there was another one, he started. He worked over Potter's Farm, t'other side of the wood.

DR KOVACS. Didn't anybody tell you it was wrong, what they were doing?

EFFIE. My mum and dad done it.

DR KOVACS. Yes, but . . .

EFFIE. I seem em doing it.

DR KOVACS. I suppose so.

EFFIE. Didn't think about it. T'was just how it was. And that feller from Potter's Farm, he give me sweeties. He give me a ribbon once. 'Where'd you get that,' my dad said? 'Found it.' I said. In the wood.

DR KOVACS. So you did know it was wrong?

EFFIE. Don't know. Say 'Where'd you get that?'

DR KOVACS. Where did you get that?

EFFIE. No. No. In a bad voice.

DR KOVACS (*in a voice of authority that startles both of them*). Where did you get that?

EFFIE (*automatic response*). Found it. (*Pause.*) See. Frightened me. So I told a lie. Found it. (*A pause.*) So then it starts to get fat. Like that. And my dad says, ''Cos she eats too much'. And my mum thinks: No, it ent, and she took me down her sister's and she says: 'Is it what I think, Cissie?' And they dug their fingers in. Like that. And she says, 'Yes, tis'. And my mum says, 'Oh God, ow'm I going to tell him,

Ciss?' And she says, 'Effie, who done that to you?' And my aunty says, 'Tis no good. She don't know what you mean. She'm too daft.' My mum says, 'Effie, have any men come along and took your drawers off and done them sort of things to you?' And I says 'Yes'. And my aunty she says 'Win, you'll have to do summat with her'.

And then we goes home and my mum's crying and saying 'Oh God, ow'm I going to tell him?' And my dad . . . my dad says 'Effing brat. Underneath the field hedges with any old dirty bugger that comes sniffin' round. Got a name now for it, ent she? Any bugger wants it, go'n find Effie Palmer. She'll give it yer.'

And then after that . . . (*She frowns in a muddled, vague way as if uncertain quite what did happen after that.*) . . . after that they comes for me in the van. My dad says I was out of control. He said he was going to beat I. 'Bloody flay her alive,' he said. So I shut myself up in my cupboard and I held on to the door when anyone come. My dad said, 'Leave her, Win. She'll come out when she'm hungry'. But I wouldn't come out, see. I wouldn't. And they come and they pulled open the door and I screamed and I kicked and they pushed me into the van and they sat on me. I couldn't breathe, Miss.

And my mum's face was like stone. Watching. (*A long pause.*)

DR KOVACS. What happened to the baby?

EFFIE. What?

DR KOVACS. The baby?

EFFIE. What baby?

DR KOVACS. Your baby.

EFFIE (*vaguely*). I don't know. Don't remember.

DR KOVACS. You don't remember the baby being born?

EFFIE (*after some thought*). Yes. Remember that. Remember the pain. (*More thought.*) T'was a little girl.

DR KOVACS. What happened to her, Effie?

EFFIE. Dunno.

DR KOVACS. Did you ask?

EFFIE. 'Can't have a baby living here, Effie, can we? Crampton Court's no proper place for a baby, is it? We'll find a nice home for her.'
Don't remember.

DR KOVACS. Oh, Effie . . .

EFFIE. I'm tired now, Miss. (*They are both lost in thought. Then* DR KOVACS *makes a move.*) Will you come tomorrow, Miss?

DR KOVACS. Yes.

EFFIE (*surprised*). You crying, Miss?

DR KOVACS. No. Just . . . (*As she comes out, helplessly, to the audience.*) Just . . . (*She struggles hard not to cry. Some hair is falling down. She pins it up.*) Just . . .
Do you know, I think if I were not under strict control all the time . . . all the time . . . if I once let one half of what's in here out, then the ceilings would crack, the floors would open, the roofs fly off slate by slate into the air, girders buckle, pavements open up, forests rip apart and swirl into the clouds, the seas boil, the skies grow black . . . (*She gathers herself back under control.*) As it is, however, I keep the surfaces smooth and cover up the pain. It's the only way. The only way.

Play Sources and Acknowledgements

Anne Boleyn by Peter Albery (in *Plays of the Year 1955–6*, ed. JC Trewin. Paul Elek). Copyright © 1956 by Peter Albery. Reprinted by permission of Sylvia Fry.

The Cuckoo Sister by Vivien Alcock (Methuen Children's Books). Copyright © 1985 by Vivien Alcock. Reprinted by permission of Reed Consumer Books Ltd.

The Sea by Edward Bond (in *Bond Plays: Two*, Methuen World Classics). Copyright © 1973 by Edward Bond. Reprinted by permission of Reed Consumer Books Ltd.

Skungpoomery by Ken Campbell (Methuen Young Drama). Copyright © 1980 by Ken Campbell. Reprinted by permission of Reed Consumer Books Ltd.

Split Down the Middle by David Campton (unpublished script). Copyright © 1965 by David Campton, 35 Liberty Road, Leicester LE3 8JF. Reprinted by permission of the author.

Top Girls by Caryl Churchill (Methuen Student Edition; Methuen Modern Plays; and in *Churchill Plays: Two*, Methuen World Classics). Copyright © 1982 by Caryl Churchill. Reprinted by permission of Reed Consumer Books Ltd.

Easy Virtue by Noel Coward (in *Coward Plays: One*, Methuen World Classics). Copyright © 1926 by Noel Coward. Reprinted by permission of the Estate of Noel Coward by arrangement with Michael Imison Playwrights Ltd.

223

224